BETTER OFF DEAD

Post-Traumatic Stress
Disorder *and the* Canadian
Armed Forces

FRED DOUCETTE

NIMBUS
PUBLISHING
NIMBUS.CA

Nimbus Publishing Limited
3731 Mackintosh St, Halifax, NS B3K 5A5
(902) 455-4286 nimbus.ca

Printed and bound in Canada
NB1211
Cover photo: Alamy Images, BDAA6B
Cover Design: Heather Bryan
Interior Design: JVDW Designs

Library and Archives Canada Cataloguing in Publication

Doucette, Fred, author
Better off dead : post-traumatic stress disorder and the
Canadian Armed Forces / Fred Doucette.

Issued in print and electronic formats.
ISBN 978-1-77108-354-6 (paperback).—ISBN 978-1-77108-355-3 (html)

1. Doucette, Fred. 2. War neuroses—Canada. 3. Post-traumatic stress disorder—Canada. 4. Veterans—Mental health—Canada. 5. Soldiers—Mental health—Canada. 6. Veterans—Mental health services—Canada. 7. Soldiers—Mental health services—Canada. 8. Canada—Armed Forces—Medical care. 9. Medicine, Military—Canada. I. Title.

RC550.D68 2015   616.85'212   C2015-904325-5
                                 C2015-904326-3

Nimbus Publishing acknowledges the financial support for its publishing activities from the Government of Canada through the Canada Book Fund (CBF) and the Canada Council for the Arts, and from the Province of Nova Scotia. We are pleased to work in partnership with the Province of Nova Scotia to develop and promote our creative industries for the benefit of all Nova Scotians.

"The military mind will not, perhaps does not dare, admit that there comes a time to every fighting man (unless death or bloody ruination of the flesh forestalls it) when the Worm—not steel and flame—becomes his nemesis."

—Farley Mowat, *And No Birds Sang*

CONTENTS

FOREWORD

Canadian soldiers have always been war-fighters. They bring their knowledge, discipline, and professionalism to some of the most dangerous places in the world. They carry our values in their hearts and minds, and are not immune to the horror of conflict—or the invisible wounds of Post-Traumatic Stress Disorder (PTSD) that have followed it through the ages. *Better Off Dead* is a powerful account of how Canadian society has failed its soldiers and veterans suffering from PTSD. A highly respected leader and courageous soldier, author Fred Doucette provides raw reports of soldiers' search for understanding and support—some successful and, sadly, others tragic. He is one of the pioneers blazing the trail in bringing operational stress injury from darkness into the light, and his experiences, and the stories he tells of others, are real and insightful.

With well over forty years of experience with the Canadian Armed Forces (CAF), Fred has worked for the last decade as a peer support coordinator with the Canadian Forces Operational Stress Injury Social Support (OSISS) Program. He has helped soldiers and others deal with the storms of emotion that push them into a deep state of depression, where demons own their hearts and they truly think they would be better off dead. He has witnessed how families suffer when the ugliness of war invades the mind of a soldier. And he is also able to provide precious insights into the RCMP, and the issues of sexual assault and suicide.

The end of UN Peacekeeping, NATO interventions, and coalition missions have caused today's mental wounds. Fred reminds us that the CAF needs to mature swiftly and appreciate the relationship between physical and psychological health. He inspires us to consider a total-person concept and to respect that PTSD is a valid injury that desperately requires education and understanding now. *Better Off Dead* offers rich insights for all leaders in the CAF and Veterans Affairs as well as first-responder organizations including the RCMP. By embracing the lessons shared by Fred and others, you too could be rewarded, as Fred frequently was, by having someone say to you, "You saved my life."

Pro Patria!

Peter Devlin
Lieutenant-General (Retired)
July 2015

PREFACE

It's 4:30 P.M. on a Thursday and another therapy session is over. Nothing earth-shattering discovered or resolved, just the familiar uneasy feeling I get when we've been working on some of the deeply buried memories. My "psycho sessions" with my "psycho lady" have been part of life for the past ten years. Most of my recovery from post-traumatic stress disorder (PTSD) was achieved in my first two years of therapy. For the past eight years my regular sessions have been part of the self-care regimen required by my job while working as a peer support coordinator with the Canadian Forces Operational Stress Injury Social Support Program (OSISS). The sessions allow me to download some of the vicarious trauma and stress that I encounter when dealing with soldiers and veterans who are suffering from an operational stress injury (OSI), with PTSD being one of the most common of these.

Finishing my therapy at 4:30 usually puts me in the Fredericton rush half-hour—the city isn't big enough to have a full-fledged rush hour. Today I was stopped at a street light waiting to turn left when I noticed a dad and his son crossing the street. Watching the little fellow's wobbly gait I figured he was about two years old and he seemed overjoyed to be out with his dad. He wore a sky-blue toque, red mittens, and snow boots that went up to his knees and looked too big for his little legs and feet. He reminded me of my grandson Logan who is just shy of two years old and proud as punch that he can get around on his own little legs.

The little guy and his dad made it across the street, my light changed, and I made my turn. I was abreast of them and took one more look at the little fellow. Then it was as if everything slipped into slow motion as the little boy turned his head towards me and looked me straight in the eyes. His face was a picture of innocence, his eyes were dark, and in them I imagined a look of fear. Those eyes caught me off guard and tripped a trigger that I thought I had under control. In an instant I was awash in a flood of anxiety and fear for this unknown child. It was a look I had seen a hundred times before in Bosnia and it was now unlocking a door to memories I feared. My breathing became short, I could feel the rush of adrenaline hit the way it used to in Bosnia when I had to deal with incidents involving kids. My stomach felt as if it had rolled over, my grip on the steering wheel tightened, my vision drew in and focused on what was in front of me—everything else was grey. I was heading towards a full-blown flashback and I knew I had to get a grip on it before it got me.

As if possessed, I began yelling, "Don't let it get you, don't let it get you, you're in Fredericton on your way home, the kid is OK, you're not in Bosnia, your grandkids are OK, they're safe, you're in Canada not Bosnia, everyone is safe, you are going home to supper, it's OK, Fred, it's OK, Fred." An overwhelming rush of emotion came over me like a hot flash, my eyes started to tear up and a feeling of gut-wrenching grief hit me as I imagined what it would be like to lose someone dear to mè, especially a child. My mantra had kept the flashback at bay, but now I was wrapped in an emotional dive.

"Breathe, Fred," I said out loud. "In through the nose, hold it, breathe out through the mouth, relax your grip, everyone is OK, think of the good not the evil, they're safe. Keep breathing, you'll see them grow into adults, no one will harm them." I felt my grip loosen and my vision widen. I kept mumbling positive words as I made my way home. Stopping at our mailbox I got out and gulped in fresh air as if I had almost drowned. I guess drowning is a good analogy when it comes to explaining what had just happened to me. It is as if you are fifty feet underwater and you have only enough air to make it halfway up. You're looking up and you can see the light of the surface but you lose strength and weaken, it gets darker, and you're dumped into your little piece of hell again.

I arrived home exhausted. These episodes when they occur, which thankfully is not very often, drain me both physically and mentally. I was glad that there was no one home when I got there. Had my wife, Janice, been home she would have easily sensed that something had happened. I got a cold drink, sat in my chair, and let the stress and tension drain out of me. I had won another battle with the memory demons; it had been a surprise attack that had caught me off guard, but thankfully my coping drills had kicked in and I had kept my head above the water.

When these storms of emotions were spinning me down into a deep state of depression I saw no reason for living, no future. In my mind the simplest solution was to be sent back. My mind had been programmed for places like Bosnia, Rwanda, and Somalia, places where the details of life are meaningless, where there are no grey areas and no one need understand why you are numb. Being numb was an asset in those places.

I didn't want to live the life I was caught up in, I wanted it to end. There were times when I thought I'd be better off dead. Take the easy way out. But whenever I thought of ending it, I either didn't have the guts or deep down I knew that I could get my life back. There were so many things I knew I needed to deal with, but I just didn't care. In military slang, my "give a fuck factor" (GAFF) was registering zero, and nothing and no one seemed important enough to care about.

Deep down, when I looked at my experiences I tried to deny that they had happened and that they were influencing my lack of drive. I thought to myself, "Fred, you're a soldier and if Bosnia got to you then the only answer is you must be weak."

What I struggled with was why and how people turn on each other and allow themselves to be drawn down into the brutal ethnic war that engulfed the Balkans. By the end of my first year at home I had devoured every book I could find about the Balkans, all in an effort to try and make sense of what I had experienced. When my pursuit of the answers started to wane, I tried to reason with myself that if I didn't care about what was going on in Bosnia then the demons would go away. However, try as I might, this strategy didn't work either. My guilt compelled me to look and listen.

By 1998 it had been two years since the war, and I still had yet to admit to myself that anything was wrong with me. The coping skills that were getting me through were pretty rough. I didn't like crowds and so my coping skill was to avoid them. I couldn't sleep and so my coping skill was to stay up late. I couldn't remember things and so my coping skill was blame someone else for not reminding me. It was all about avoidance, but that meant avoiding things that you should not avoid, like birthday gatherings, going to supper with friends, going to movies, visiting people. Deep down I didn't give a fuck about anything. The social worker on the base said that I exhibited some classic signs of PTSD, according to a questionnaire I had answered when I got back from Bosnia. Until then I had continued to deny that anything was wrong and had convinced myself that I was OK, that I just needed some adjusting and would get over it in time. I was dealing with it. In my tunnel-vision approach to life I figured if I kept telling myself that there was nothing wrong (denial is one of the first symptoms of PTSD) then the demons would go away.

So in an "Oh yeah?" moment I told Janice I would prove to her that I was OK and turned myself in to the medical system. I knew the medical officer (MO) for my unit and after a brief consultation I agreed to go to the National Defence Medical Centre (NDMC) in Ottawa for a mental health assessment. We made a deal that we would tell my bosses that it was for tests on my neck, where I had been wounded.

In June 1999 I flew to Ottawa to the Post Traumatic Stress Disorder Clinic, where I met with a civilian psychiatrist. He was forty-five minutes late and arrived from his extended lunch picking at his teeth with a toothpick. I was not impressed. I spent about forty-five minutes with him, he asked a bunch of canned questions, and I decided that he knew jack shit about where I had served and what I had experienced. Energized by mistrust, I easily picked up on his persistence to get two questions in particular answered; the two that confirmed my opinion that the PTSD clinic is sham, whose sole purpose was to protect the system and not help soldiers:

"Do you want to hurt anyone, family, friends, et cetera?" and "Are you looking for compensation from the Crown [actual words] in the form of a medical pension?"

What a fucking crock of shit, I thought, I'm out of here. He seemed shocked when I got up and walked out of his office. In the taxi on the way to the airport I kept thinking that this was all about protecting politicians and leadership and fuck the troops. I was so angry at them and at the system. I didn't want much, just some acknowledgement of the pact that is supposed to exist between a country and its soldiers, to the effect of "We sent you to war and now that you are hurt we will take care of you like we are supposed to." When I got back from Ottawa I knew I was descending deeper into my black hole. I was meandering through life in a fog with my demons swirling my head. I was asking a God that I didn't believe in to just end it now.

I had hit a wall and one day Janice had had enough. She cornered me, looked me in the eye, and said, "Fred, you need help." I think it was the first time anyone had said that to me. For some reason, her words that day cut through all of my bullshit and I said OK. In June of 2000 I went to Halifax for an assessment. The assessment would be simple: I'd spend a couple of days telling them about my experiences and their effect on me. I didn't understand how they were going to assess the damage done, nail down the diagnosis, and prescribe a treatment all in a day and a half. I remember being anxious and afraid of what they would tell me.

My appointment spanned the 5th and 6th of June. On the first day I was screened by a psychologist, and the following day was given my diagnosis by a psychiatrist. I had to physically and mentally force myself to stay focused on my commitment to pursuing a balance in my life. At the end of the first day I felt so fucking exhausted, I had nothing left in me. I wanted to crawl into a hole and never come out. There was so much there. Memories that only came in the loneliness of night or the flashbacks that grabbed me in the light of day and transported me back to the sights, sounds, smells, angers, fears, hopelessness, guilt, confusion, hatred, heartache, tears...of a city at war.

On day two I met with the psychiatrist who diagnosed me with severe chronic PTSD. I would be put on medication, start therapy, and get to work on coming back to the real world. I wanted my next twenty years to be free of the demons. I didn't want these experiences to rule my life and haunt me to my grave.

In 1994 I was placed on standby to deploy overseas as a UN Military Observer (UNMO). On the July 5, 1995, I deployed to Croatia and several days later I made my way into the besieged Bosnian city of Sarajevo. In hindsight this was the beginning of the end of the Fred I had been for forty-three years. I was wounded on July 17, 1995, in Sarajevo, Bosnia-Herzegovina, and I arrived home in July 1996. In June 2000 I was diagnosed with severe chronic PTSD. Under the Universality of Service it was determined that I was no longer fit to serve and I was medically released from the Canadian Armed Forces in 2002.

During my years of service I had been on six foreign missions: four in Bosnia and two in Cyprus. I had also served on several domestic operations such as Oka and the Swissair Flight 111 recovery. I had joined as a private in the infantry and was released as a captain.

Upon my release I was approached and offered a job with the newly launched Operational Stress Injury Social Support (OSISS) program. I dealt with serving soldiers and veterans by "listening, assessing, and referring" them to mental health organizations for diagnosis and therapy. For several years I dealt mainly with those who had served in Bosnia, Rwanda, Kosovo, Cyprus, the Middle East, Somalia, Ethiopia, Haiti, and the Congo. However, eventually those with service in Afghanistan would be our main "peer" source.

I can summarize my ten years with OSISS by saying that dealing with the soldiers and veterans was the easy part of the job. Dealing with the Canadian Armed Forces and Veterans Affairs was extremely frustrating and demoralizing. Those veterans and soldiers who stepped forward were the pioneers who blazed a trail which has brought OSIS from the darkness into the light where it is accepted by most that these are injuries related to military service.

The system was not ready for the onslaught of psychologically wounded soldiers, especially those from operations in Afghanistan. Soldiers still do not trust the system, especially since the Universality of Service explicitly states that you must be able to perform your job without restrictions and deploy on operations. We called psychological trauma the "kiss of death" because it likely meant the end of your career. Knowing this, many soldiers refuse to get help for their psychological injuries.

After ten years with OSISS I had no more left to give. I was burnt out and my own mental health began to suffer. My frustration with the system did not improve. The CAF, Veterans Affairs, and the medical system were already stressed to the limit. The mental health system could not cope with the numbers of psychologically injured veterans and soldiers. In 2002 the entirety of mental health resources for Base Gagetown was made up of two psychologists, a social worker, a mental health nurse, and a clerk.

This book tells the stories of serving soldiers and veterans and their struggles to get their lives back. Their honesty is beyond reproach and I feel honoured that they have allowed me to share their experiences here.

INTRODUCTION

History has called it soldier's heart, shell shock, combat fatigue, combat stress, battle fatigue, and post-traumatic stress disorder. They are all the same: invisible wounds. PTSD has a history as significant as the malady itself. It's been with us now for thousands of years, as incidents in history have proved beyond a doubt.

During World War I, the horrors and brutality of war were brought to an industrial level, and with that came the realization that battle fatigue plays no favorites: all ranks in combat units are vulnerable, from troopers to commanding officers.

For the combat soldier, the mental collapse was known as shell shock. At first, most doctors thought it was a physical ailment brought on by exploding shells. Front-line medical officers did not know what to do with shell-shocked soldiers. The worst cases, men who could not speak or walk, or who screamed uncontrollably, were sent to the rear. The cry from the leadership safe and away from the horror of the trenches was "Get them back into the line." The military remained skeptical about the legitimacy of shell shock as an illness.

At the beginning and throughout World War II military officers rejected the advice of psychiatrists, insisting that exhaustion casualties would not be a significant. However, the numbers told a different story: between July 21 and August 30, 1944, 3,000 Canadians were killed and 7,000 wounded. More than 1,500 exhaustion cases were evacuated beyond the regimental aid posts.

After World War II there was little interest in psychiatric casualties and many veterans ended up self-medicating with alcohol and drugs. The number that ended up in prison, mental institutions, or in extreme cases committed suicide was never documented. In Canada, the Royal Canadian Legions thrived as returning veterans found the legion to be the place to go for a beer and a gabfest.

My father-in-law, James Wiper, a veteran who served overseas and was wounded twice, has never stepped into a legion hall. He told me, "Most of the men who hung out at the legion either never saw action or they had saw too much and needed the drink to keep the memories at bay." Like the majority of veterans, he just wanted to forget. Regardless of wanting, my wife, Janice, told me that as a child she sometimes heard her dad talking in his sleep. She lay in the dark wondering why her dad talked in a voice she had never heard before during the daytime. She now knows it was his war voice and that it meant he was caught up in nightmares that never went away.

My father and several uncles served during World War II, but they rarely talked about the war other than to share some of the humorous times they'd had overseas. When they would get together for a few beers I'd hang around and listen to their stories and laugh with them. Most times I didn't know what I was laughing at; it just seemed like the thing to do. There were times, though, when someone would say something and they would all become silent, lost in some collective memory. Were they remembering the war, I thought? The trance usually only lasted seconds and most times it was broken by the unconscious raising of a beer. They always looked a bit embarrassed after zoning out. They'd recover by saying things like, "Yeah, yeah, and a nice fellow, too bad. He didn't make it, I miss him." Then with a collective pull on their beers they would be back in safer territory. "Do you remember the time we got in shit for taking the pie from the officer's kitchen?"

Over time I have come to understand why the booze flowed like water with my dad's generation: it was medicine. The legion halls all over the country were full of men who just wanted to forget. Getting pissed with your mates and remembering those who never came home shrouded the guilt of having survived.

In 1956 we moved from Amherst, Nova Scotia, to Montreal and my dad got a job at Reliable Steel, a scrapyard on St. Patrick Street in Pointe-Saint-Charles. We lived in the flat above the scrapyard office. Right across the street was a railyard which was separated from a lumberyard and the Lachine Canal by a small wooded strip of land. In that small strip of woods is where we regularly fought the French kids because the rail yard, woods, lumberyard, and canal were on the French side of the Pointe. The fights were for possession of that strip of shrubbery, the best place to hang out.

My first sight of a rubbie was in "our" little forest. I had seen man nests before amongst the shrubberies in the woods, with a piece of cardboard laid out on the ground, the remnants of a small fire, and empty bottles strewn about, but I had never seen anyone around them so they never meant anything to me. It was midsummer and the days were long which meant we didn't need to be home until around ten o'clock. One night three of us decided to go and watch the canal boats from the top of a lumber pile.

We were ducking through the woods when we heard someone yell, "Fuck off, you little fuckers!" Being little, we knew it was meant for us. We took to our heels like the little fuckers we were. We went to ground on top of a lumber pile and, being kids, we could not resist checking out who was down there. There were three men sitting around a small fire, dressed in old army greatcoats, bundled up like they were expecting it to snow. They were

XX BETTER OFF DEAD

talking but we couldn't hear what they were saying and one of the men was clutching a bottle.

"Rubbies, what's a rubbie?"

"You know, guys that drink rubbing alcohol."

"My dad told me it's cheaper than real booze and stronger."

A couple of months later as I was walking along St. Patrick Street, I noticed a rubbie pushing a small hand cart made from a wooden shipping crate and two baby-carriage wheels. He wore no hat, his hair was dark, dirty, long, and so greasy it shone. He wore an old army coat that went down well below his knees. The coat was tied around his waist with a piece of baler twine. He walked fast, his loose boots clomping with each step, and every few steps he'd look to his left, right, and behind as if looking for someone or something. I kept my distance but followed him around the corner onto Ropery Street where he turned in to the huge open gate of Bedard's Scrapyard. The scrap was weighed and their transaction ended as the scrapyard guy handed over a couple of bucks, and without even looking at the money the rubbie stuffed it into his pocket, turned, and left. Like a typical kid with an attention span of seconds, I too turned and carried on to my friend's house. At my friend's place we sat on the stoop and whiled away the morning doing not much of anything. At one point our gabbing settled on the subject of the rubbies and about our run-in with them and I told him about the rubbie I had seen at Bedard's that morning.

My friend's mom was sitting in the kitchen just down the hall from us, puffing on a rollie and sipping a cup of tea. She must have overheard us and said, "What about rubbies? Ah, you little friggers [Catholic for fuckers], I hope you haven't been bugging them!" No, we were just wondering who they were, they all seemed to look the same.

My friend's mom got up from the table and joined us on the stoop with her tea, her ever-present cigarette dangling from the corner of her mouth. She took a lung-filling drag and without taking the cigarette out of her mouth exhaled a huge cloud of smoke and said, "I'll tell you who those men are."

She surprised me when she said they were soldiers.

Soldiers?

"Yes, they're sick soldiers."

Why are they sick?

"They went to war."

When?

"The Second World War, and they saw and did things that no man should see or do." She paused, took another drag on her smoke, exhaled, and in an angry tone said, "Even though the war has been over for fifteen years, they still can't forget what they saw and did."

War, I thought, we won the war so why are they sick? What did they see and do?

"Never mind, you'll learn more when you grow up. Just remember these fellows gave everything so we can live and be safe today."

I asked her why they drank rubbing alcohol. "It's cheaper than store-bought booze and it's a lot stronger." But why do they drink? She didn't answer as she took a drag from her cigarette, took it out of her mouth, held it between her nicotine-stained fingers, took a sip of her tea, and with a faraway look of memories still too close to home, said, "To forget to forget." She stood up, stepped into the hallway, and closed the door behind her, leaving me with more questions than answers.

CHAPTER 1

BETTER OFF DEAD

A t the time of this incident Ted was home on sick leave. In 2002 weeks and months of sick leave was the norm for soldiers with an operational stress injury. But in many cases being home and alone caused more damage than good: soldiers felt forgotten and that no one cared.

After a bad night of fighting insomnia followed by a fitful sleep and vivid nightmares, Ted sat in his kitchen drinking coffee feeling that it was time for him to make a decision. By mid-morning he was spiraling down into the depths of depression and anxiety and he knew where it was taking him. This was not the first time he had come close to attempting suicide, but thankfully so far he had been able to resist the urge to end it all.

Terrified and paranoid with anxiety, he made his way onto the base and to the medical clinic. All he was looking for was help. Arriving at the clinic he went to reception and explained to the medic what was going on: "I need help. I am suicidal." The medic said, "Go have a seat in the waiting room and we'll get to you." Ted was dressed in a T-shirt and sweatpants; everyone else in the waiting room was in uniform. He was emotional to the point of tears and quickly became the focus of attention of the other soldiers in the waiting room. So there's Ted, a depressed individual in a suicidal panic state, suffering from severe paranoia, being stared at by fit soldiers in uniform.

He was too embarrassed to even raise his head. At 1200 he was told to go have lunch and be back by 1300. He stayed where he was, lost in the nightmare that was swirling around in his head. Lunch came and went and by 1500 he had had enough. He took his sick chit and wrote on it "I'm going to kill myself." Then he threw it into the basket and walked out.

At home he took some medication, buried himself in bed, and with the voice in his head repeating "I'd be better off dead," passed out.

He awoke at 0300, and noticed that his wife had come home from work and was asleep beside him. Still dressed in what he called his "give up on life clothes"—sweatpants, T-shirt, and running shoes—he decided that it was time.

He went outside, got in his car, and as he backed of the driveway he said goodbye to his wife and daughter. He drove to the Catholic church on the base, parked his car, got out, and sat on the steps. He sat there holding the butcher knife he had taken from home. He stared at the reflection of the streetlights on the blade of the knife and he felt a sense of calm and contentment come over him. He was not afraid to die. He would be free from his misery and his wife and daughter would be better off without him.

He was amazed at how his senses became clear in that moment. The warmth of the night, the mild breeze, the smell of the flowers by the church, the silence. It all felt so comfortable; it was like his brain was taking it all in for the last time. He had made the decision to die and with that the voice that had relentlessly tortured him was gone, apparently satisfied that it had succeeded.

His first-aid training had taught him where the bleeders were. 'I'll slash my arms, lay back, and let my life flow out of me,' he thought. He leaned back and was taking in the night sky. He jumped. His cell phone was ringing. The ringing was so loud it snapped him out of his trance and he automatically answered it.

"Honey, where are you? I got up to go to the bathroom and you're not in the house...what's going on?"

"Nothing, dear, I just needed some fresh air. I'll be home in a minute." Her call had broken the trance. All it took was for someone to show they cared about him.

Ted's wife never found out that her call had saved his life that warm summer night. The next day, fed up with the base medical clinic and without their referral, he went and admitted himself to the regional hospital. He ended up spending several weeks there being treated and cared for by civilian practitioners.

I visited Ted several times when he was in the hospital and when told me his story I was livid. I went in to see the base health administrator and told him what had occurred. He seemed confused when I asked him, "Do you have a protocol for a heart attack?"

"Of course. Any chest pain and we automatically hook them up to an EKG."

"I see. And what happens if a soldier walks in and has accidently chopped a finger off?"

"Well, we get right at it with an x-ray, sutures, and so on."

"Now, riddle me this one, Batman," I said. "What the fuck is your protocol for a soldier arriving in a state of severe psychological distress to the point of saying he/she wants to kill themselves?"

Silence.

I was livid, ready to lose it, so I paused and said, "You don't have one, do you? No need to reply, because you don't have an answer, right, you have an excuse? Don't say a word, because I don't want to hear the bullshit. It is your responsibility to make sure that there is a drill to care for those soldiers that are suffering from a mental health injury. Fuck, this injured soldier sat there totally ignored as soldiers with colds, sprains, and other crap were seen before him and in the end after several hours of waiting he thought, 'Fuck it, no one cares,' and he left. Your staff had an opportunity to intervene in a suicide, to care for an injured soldier...to save his life. So why don't you do something about it...right!"

Not expecting an answer I walked out of his office. Another minute in there looking at his dumb face and I would have smashed him.

The solution was so simple: all they had to do was do their jobs. Nothing changed after that first visit. Naively, I thought we might be called in to brief on OSIS and enlighten or, better still, sensitize the medical staff to the plight of their peers suffering mental health injuries. The call never came. In the ten years I was the peer support coordinator I was never once asked to brief the staff at the base medical clinic. They were the experts and no one was going to tell them how to do their job.

Ted was released from the regional hospital after a month and medically released from the CF several months later. He and his family moved back to Nova Scotia soon after. A friend of mine there told me Ted is working full-time and doing extremely well.

CHAPTER 2

WHAT'S WRONG WITH ME?

Bob was the first veteran I met with when I started working for the Operational Stress Injury Social Support Program (OSISS). I received a call from "Chipper" Christensen, Regimental Sergeant Major (RSM) of the 2nd Battalion of the Royal Canadian Regiment (RCR). He had just got off the phone with Bob's wife, Joanne, who was at her wits' end trying to get help for Bob. The RSM had asked her if she would like to talk with me to see if I could help. She agreed.

I had only just finished the two-week peer support course and not had the time to set up a game plan as to how I would handle a request for help. This request was even more difficult because it was the spouse of a veteran who was reaching out for help. Did Bob know, and was he really receptive to having me visit? Or was his wife forcing him to seek help, which could make things really difficult? I had an imagined list of what-ifs running through my head, none of which fit the situation. I had no excuse not to call, so I dialled the number.

When Joanne answered, I introduced myself and gave her my spiel about the OSISS program. She didn't sound too confident with the ball she had got rolling, which made me feel more acutely that I was treading on unknown ground. When I finally shut up, she still seemed a bit guarded and I couldn't blame her. The line was silent so finally I asked her, "How are you doing and how is Bob?" Several years of pent up emotion, frustration, anger, confusion, and not knowing what to do to help the man she loved poured out. I listened intently and between the tears and sniffling it struck me that she could have been talking about how *I* was two years ago.

Bob had served over twenty years in the army as an infantry-man in the Royal Canadian Regiment and the Canadian Airborne Regiment. He had retired as a warrant officer (WO) a few years ago, and was now unemployed and drowning in the depths of what would eventually be diagnosed as PTSD. When I had accepted this job I had promised myself that I would do whatever needed to be done to get a veteran or soldier the help they needed. I also made it my own policy that I would not meet a peer on the phone. I would meet them face to face. Joanne said she doubted Bob would meet with me let alone talk to me on the phone.

She told me that he had hour-long bouts of crying, he was jittery, his hands trembled, and he was frightened of everything and everyone. Choking back tears, Joanne said he was embarrassed: the hard-nosed airborne infantry warrant officer was now an emotional wreck and he didn't want anyone to see him in this state. In my years with OSISS I would find out that what most people who need help just wanted to be asked was "How are you doing?" followed by "How can I help?"

Joanne promised me that she would ask Bob if it would be OK for me to drop by for a coffee. The ball was in his court and all he had to do was hit it back. Joanne phoned me a week later and said that Bob was willing to meet with me, but was too embarrassed to call. She told me to come by the next day. I almost told her that I was probably just as nervous as Bob, this being my first visit with a peer. I did the wise thing and kept quiet about that. I told her I'd be over around ten o'clock.

Bob and Joanne live about twenty minutes from Fredericton in the rural community of Rusagonis. On my way there I kept rehearsing my spiel. I was nervous, and had doubts as to whether I could help or not. I figured if I introduced myself and the program that it would be a good icebreaker, not just for Bob, but for me. I kept reminding myself that we had both been soldiers and spoke the language of soldiering. Remember: just relax and listen, I told myself. I pulled into the driveway and sat there for a moment getting psyched up. I took a few deep breaths to release the tension and said to myself, Let's get on with this. As I walked towards the door all I could think of was, What the fuck are you doing? I approached the door with trepidation and knocked. The door opened and it was showtime.

"Hi, Joanne, I'm Fred Doucette." I shook her hand and stepped into the kitchen. Bob was sitting at the table, his hands wrapped around a coffee mug, staring into it and avoiding eye contact with me. "Hi, Bob."

He raised his head, stood up, and looked me in the eye. Then he reached out and shook my hand and in a nervous voice said, "Fred, nice to see you. Coffee?"

"Yes, thanks, that sounds good."

It would be good to wrap my hands around a cup of coffee, like Bob had been doing, so I wouldn't fidget, a safe place to look when things inevitably went silent. Bob busied himself making the coffee while Joanne put some cookies on a plate and placed them on the table. I looked around the cozy, warm kitchen. Like so many Maritime kitchens it was the centre of the home, a comfortable place to sit and socialize. But at that moment there was nothing comfortable about being in the kitchen; you could feel the tension in the room as the three of us wondered how this was going to play out. Bob didn't realize it, but he'd taken the first and hardest step in getting his life back. He had reached out and in doing so had admitted that something had been wrong since he had returned from Bosnia.

The coffee was made, poured, and before Bob could settle into his chair I launched into my over-rehearsed intro. "The Operational Stress Injury Social Support Program started last year as a partial response to the growing number of veterans and soldiers who have returned from operations with a psychological injury...Blah, blah, blah....We help veterans and soldiers blah, blah, we're 100 percent confidential...blah, blah, we listen, assess, and refer. We are non-medical...blah, blah, we're a shoulder to lean on as you recover, and finally, we have all served on overseas missions and have been diagnosed with PTSD." As I spoke I had a chance to take a good look at Bob and saw that there was no reaction when I said psychological injury. He looked shattered, tired, nervous, anxious, and embarrassed. He had hit the wall.

There comes a point with PTSD when you hit the wall by yourself and finally choose or are forced to reach out for help. The wall comes in many forms and it can spring up at any time. In a perfect world the simplest wall would be if, a couple of months after your return from a mission, you realize you are not well and you seek help. However, that rarely happens and most will first face family problems, domestic violence, problems at work, family break up, drug, alcohol, or gambling addictions, release from the military, acute mental breakdown, and/or attempted suicide. The ultimate wall, of course, is suicide.

Bob barely made eye contact with me and when he did it was only for a second, then he would look away. Throughout my initial spiel Bob had kept his head down, staring into his coffee cup, occasionally glancing up but not making eye contact. I could feel his embarrassment. Like most soldiers and veterans struggling with a psych injury, he was fighting the stigma attached to it. Joanne leaned across the kitchen countertop, coffee in hand, intensely focused on what was going on at the table between Bob and me. I sensed she thought I would jump up and say, "The Lord baby Jesus rise up in your soul and be healed!" But that was not going to happen because if that was all it took to be cured, I definitely would have found God by then.

Enough of the propaganda, I thought. Tell him what happened to you and the battle you've fought to try and put your demons to rest and get your life back. "Well, Bob, here is what happened to me over the past six years."

He raised his head and looked me straight in the eyes as I talked about "my Bosnia." We were on common ground now and the words and memories flowed back and forth. The dam had broken! Remember this and that, so and so, such and such, fuckin' place, people, kids, atrocities, smells, sounds, taste, fuckin' life, guilt, shame, and so on. Not details, just a common experience. The gruesomeness of what we had gone through didn't need telling. The details were in the pauses when we'd fall silent, knowing that we were in the midst of similar memories.

"Fred, I'm so angry. I can't sleep and I can't stand to be around anyone. I just want to be left alone." Glancing at Joanne. "I love her but I don't have the words to explain what I experienced or what I am going through." Joanne said little. She was simply standing by her man and I could see a tear roll down her cheek as she nodded and whispered, "I understand."

I began to relate my path back to the life I once had, and I could actually see the anxiety and stress that this visit had brought on for me slowly diminish. Bob relaxed and released his grip on his coffee mug, the tension in his face relaxed, his shoulders dropped, and the tears came. Embarrassed, he turned away and wiped his tears with a napkin. He apologized as if he had done something wrong.

"Christ, Bob, don't apologize. You're a very brave man with a wife that loves and cares about you. It's time to take care of number one and get help."

It took several minutes for the emotional armour to drop and the embarrassed tears that came with opening up to subside. I knew the feeling that came after you had finally opened up and let your emotions show. It was as if a thousand-pound cloak had been lifted off of your shoulders—it's almost euphoric. I felt relieved that we had crossed the emotional bridge between the hard soldier and the human being. I did not fully understand what had just occurred, but I had a strong feeling that, having been in Bob's shoes at one time, the buzz I felt now came from the realization that I had connected with him on an emotional level.

We sat back in our chairs, relaxed and took a deep breath, sipped our coffees. Bob began to talk. His experiences were in Bosnia in 1992 on the first UN mission to the former Yugoslavia. The UN had set up UN Protected Areas (UNPA), the main ones being Sarajevo, Srebrenica, Zepa, Gorazde, and Bihac. Bob and G Company ended up in Srebrenica surrounded by the Serbian army. The UNPAS were not protected and the Serbs pummelled them with artillery, mortars, rockets, and machine-gun fire at their leisure because the UN Rules of Engagement had no teeth. In time, the ineffective UN mandate would be totally ignored by the Serbs. Srebrenica fell in 1995. Over eight thousand men and boys were executed and buried in mass graves in the hills around the town. Regardless of the fact that Bob had not been there in 1995 when the town fell, he and many soldiers bear the guilt of what happened. Bob had kept so much in for so long that he didn't know where to start. I just let him talk, occasionally acknowledging him with an "I understand."

I was not surprised that many of his demons were the same as mine. One was the anxiety he felt when he was around other people. His solution, or, as we call it, coping skill, is quite common: to avoid people. He would walk into the woods behind his house and sit in old lawn chair for hours at a time, staring at nothing. He felt safe there. No one would ask questions about how he was doing, he wouldn't be driven to tears and have to explain himself. I told him that doing that surely worked for him but it was not a good way to cope and once he was assessed and into therapy, the psychologists would teach him how to handle his stressors in a healthier way. I can still picture Bob sitting on his chair in the woods all alone, trying to figure out what was going on with his life.

Time had raced by. Three hours had seemed like minutes. Even though I had talked with Bob about his injury and where to get help and how to plug into Veterans Affairs, I wanted to make sure that the seed had been planted and that he would seek help. I told him to see his doctor and tell him everything he had told me. One good thing was that Bob had no aversion to taking medication to help him sleep and deal with his anxiety. Many soldiers and veterans resist the need to take medication for a psychological injury because they see it as a sign of weakness. I would eventually come up with a way to get the message across:

"So, you ever injure yourself, say sprained ankle, sore back?"

"Oh yeah, I sprained my ankle parachuting."

"Did you take any meds for that?"

"Yeah, anti-inflammatories and muscle relaxants."

"Right, the anti-inflammatory to take the swelling down and muscle relaxants so you could rest and let the injury heal so you could go to physiotherapy."

"Yeah."

"After the injury healed you went to physio and the therapist started to get you to work on getting the strength back, no problem with that?"

"Nope."

"The same method is used with a mental health injury. You get assessed, the doc gives you meds so you can sleep and something to take the edge off the anger, then you start the treatment with the therapist, who is like a physiotherapist for the brain. It's the same route, just a different injury. Trust me, the meds are not going to make you drool, shit your pants. You won't have to wear a hockey helmet. I'm on meds right now!"

At the very least it made them think.

I told Bob that I would get the forms and help him sort out the paperwork for Veterans Affairs. "Once they receive the application for a disability related to your service, they will set up an appointment to get you assessed. In all likelihood the assessment will be done in Halifax at the Operational Trauma Social Support Centre. After your assessment and diagnosis you'll start therapy in Fredericton."

Short-term memory issues are the norm when you have an OSI; there is just too much to remember. I noticed that Joanne was writing things down and must have known, as I did, that Bob wouldn't remember half of what I had said.

I wasn't sure how to end my visit, but thankfully Bob did it for me. "Fred, you must be busy man. I shouldn't be keeping you." I mumbled something about having to be back at the office. We shook hands. Bob thanked me several times, as did Joanne. I said that I would be in touch the following week and that we would get the VAC paperwork underway and then I was out the door.

I took a few steps down the driveway, stopped and took a deep breath of the fresh fall air. I had survived my baptism of caring. I felt great as I drove back to Fredericton. All I could think was, Fuck, this shit works!

Bob and I met again in his kitchen a week later. He had an appointment to see his doc and we managed to get the Veterans Affairs paperwork sorted out and in the mail. I was amazed at how Bob had changed. He was smiling, upbeat, and looked rested. He had hope and he believed that he could get better and return to the life he had lost.

About a month later he headed to Halifax to be assessed and like many soldiers and veterans his recovery started the day he was diagnosed. Having the psychiatrist tell you that you have PTSD, that it's treatable, and that you will get better — just those few words make up about one-third of your recovery. In layman's terms, being able to say "I'm not going crazy" is a big step towards getting your life back. Bob told me that after several hours of assessment he was so exhausted that Joanne had to drive home. He was sound asleep before they were out of Halifax and he slept until they pulled into their driveway in Rusagonis.

Bob was a model patient. He took his meds, attended his therapy, and worked hard at getting his life back. His mental state levelled out and he has reaped the benefits of his hard work. Sadly, Bob is in the minority, when it comes to PTSD sufferers. Many have not stepped forward to be diagnosed, and in some cases those who are diagnosed are not compliant when it comes to therapy and meds.

Bob and I met several times and each time I saw him he looked stronger and healthier. I asked him about the chair in the woods and he pointed to where it now sat in the backyard with the rest of the lawn furniture. No more running and hiding, he was now Bob the veteran with an injury related to his service.

Bob got his life back, returned to work as a civilian employee with National Defence, and has never looked back. Every time we meet I can feel the positive energy just flowing out of him. He has worked his way back to the land of the living.

CHAPTER 3
THE END OF PEACEKEEPING

losely related to Canada's commitment to multilateralism has been its strong support for peacekeeping efforts. In 1947 then-Canadian diplomat Lester Pearson had an important part in founding both the United Nations and the North Atlantic Treaty Organization (NATO). Prior to Canada's role in the Suez Crisis in 1956, the country was viewed by many as insignificant in global issues. Canada's successful role in the conflict gave the country credibility and established it as a nation fighting for the "common good" of all nations. Following Suez, Canada has participated in every UN peacekeeping effort and continues to do so whenever called upon to contribute.

Since 1995, however, Canada's direct participation in UN peacekeeping efforts has greatly declined. In July 2006, for instance, Canada ranked 51st on the list of UN peacekeepers, contributing 130 peacekeepers out of a total UN deployment of over seventy thousand. That number decreased largely because Canada began to direct its participation to UN-sanctioned military operations through NATO, rather than directly to the UN.

The loss of nine Canadian peacekeepers when their Buffalo 461 was shot down over Syria in 1974 remains the largest single loss of life in Canadian peacekeeping and NATO operations including

Afghanistan. In 1988, the Nobel Peace Prize was awarded to United Nations peacekeepers, an honour which was largely ignored by the government and the media of the day.

For over forty years, Canada's claim to fame on the world stage was its participation on every peacekeeping mission mounted by the United Nations. Those of us who have served on these missions can honestly say that there has never been a successful UN mission. Every mission came with its own challenges and frustrations, no two missions were the same, and there was no template for success.

The death of peacekeeping came in the 1990s with the failed UN missions in Bosnia and Rwanda. Between Bosnia in 1992 and Rwanda in 1994, the UN failed to prevent the death of almost a million people. Peacekeepers became targets who could be brushed aside or taken hostage to be used as bargaining chips or pawns in an attempt to get concessions from the UN.

The myth that the Canadian government fed to the public was that Canadian soldiers were peacekeepers. There has never been such a thing as a peacekeeper. Canadian soldiers have always been war fighters who bring their knowledge, skills, patience, common sense, discipline, and professionalism when tasked to a UN mission. They are soldiers, who, for several months, put on a blue beret and attempt to implement a mandate put in place by the UN.

Peacekeeping provides its own stresses. Its emphasis on rules of engagement provides a containment of the roles for which soldiers are trained. Causes of stress include witnessing or experiencing the following:

- Constant tension and threat of conflict
- Threat of land mines and booby traps
- Close contact with dead people and the severely injured
- Deliberate maltreatment and atrocities, possibly involving civilians

- Cultural issues, e.g. male dominant attitudes towards women in different cultures
- Separation and home issues
- Risk of disease including HIV, Ebola, and tuberculosis, to name a few
- Threat of exposure to toxic agents
- Mission problems
- Return to service

Thousands have served and many have both the physical and mental wounds to prove it. More than 125 soldiers, seamen, and air force personnel have paid the ultimate price and given their lives while serving as peacekeepers.

It was in Bosnia that the ill-named United Nations Protection Force (UNPROFOR) would prove that the era of peacekeeping as the UN and the world once knew it was over. The UNPROFOR was composed of nearly 39,000 personnel, 320 of whom were killed on duty.

By the end of its first mandate in March 1993, UNPROFOR had had some success. However, civil unrest was such that terror, discrimination, and ethnic cleansing were still present. Humanitarian aid was disrupted due to non-cooperation and even hostile actions — mines, small arms fire, and rocket-propelled grenades (RPG) — toward the parties on the field, especially from the Bosnian Serb forces.

Overt hostilities against the UN forces were constant. One of the Canadian soldiers killed in Bosnia was targeted and hit square in the chest by an RPG designed to penetrate a tank's armour. Soldiers who witnessed it said he disappeared in a "pink mist." What was left of him was gathered up, put into a body bag, and shipped home to his family in a small town in Quebec.

The government of the day didn't want the public to know that Canadian soldiers were being killed and wounded on a peacekeeping mission, so to ease the family's grief they told them he was killed in a vehicle accident. It was not until some of his friends who were in Bosnia with him arrived home several months after his death and paid a visit to his family that the truth came out. The troops were astounded when the family asked them, "Was it a bad accident that killed our son?"

"What accident? Didn't they tell you he was killed by a Serb soldier?" The soldiers told the family that it would be bad press for the government, especially when Canadians were being told that Bosnia was a UN peacekeeping mission. There was no peace to keep in Bosnia, and Canadian soldiers were stuck in the middle of a horrific war with the power to do very little, other than serve as targets.

From March 1993, Serb paramilitary units on a systematic campaign of terror killed a great number of civilians, destroyed habitations, prevented the UN High Commission for Refugees (UNHCR) from delivering humanitarian aid, and forced thousands of Bosniak (a term for Muslim Bosnians) refugees to flee to Srebrenica. In Srebrenica, thirty or forty people were dying daily from military action, starvation, exposure to cold, or lack of medical treatment.

On May 26, 1995, following NATO air raids on Pale as the Bosnian Serbs defied another UN ultimatum on heavy weapons, around four hundred peacekeeping troops were taken hostage, brought to strategic points as human shields, and shown in chains on Serbian TV. The Serbs were determined to make a point to the wider world.

The peacekeepers, massively outnumbered, had to surrender after brief symbolic fights. In several instances, UN soldiers were surrounded in weapon storage areas by massively superior Serbian forces. The Serbs had given the UN and the world the finger, and knowing that there were no immediate consequences to the genocide they were conducting, they carried on with the ethnic cleansing of Bosnia.

In July 1995 Serb troops, under general Ratko Mladić, occupied the UN "safe area" of Srebrenica in eastern Bosnia and killed around 8,000 men (most women were expelled to Bosniak-held territory where some of them were raped and killed). The action taken by the Serbs was ruled as genocide and a crime against humanity. By 2006, forty-two mass graves had been uncovered around Srebrenica and specialists believe there are twenty-two more. The work of recovering was tedious: 2,070 victims were identified while body parts in more than 7,000 bags still awaited identification. On August 11, 2006 over 1,000 body parts were exhumed from one of Srebrenica's mass graves located in Kamenica.

Early in September 1995, NATO had had enough of the UN's attempt at sorting out Bosnia and began intensive wide-ranging air strikes against Bosnian Serb infrastructure and units through the first half of September. The mood in the city was "When is it going to start again?" No one trusted ceasefires. There had been thirty-two of them over the duration of the war and for the most part, they never lasted more than a few days. But this one did, and those of us stationed in Bosnia began to think that maybe the war was over.

The Serbs were bombed into attending the Dayton, Ohio, peace talks and on November 21, 1995, the Dayton Accord was agreed to. What followed was the deployment of the NATO-led Implementation Force (IFOR) on December 20, 1995 to ensure the adherence of the Former Warring Factions (FWF) to the Agreement for Peace in Bosnia and Herzegovina. I took off my blue UN beret and donned my Canadian green beret and moved north to work with a British unit. The NATO Implementation Force which deployed into Bosnia would serve as a template on intervention into other "hot spots" such as Kosovo.

The UN mission in the former Yugoslavia was particularly difficult for those deployed there. The human atrocities perpetrated against the civilian population were horrific and UN troops witnessed human brutality on a scale not seen in Europe since World War II.

I have come believe that there is nothing more destructive to the human psyche than being able to help someone in need but being prevented from doing so.

Whenever I briefed soldiers, veterans, or the public about PTSD resulting from peacekeeping missions, I used an example involving soldiers deployed to Bosnia in 1993. Frustrating, heart-wrenching, angry situations were the norm for the Balkan war that raged for three years in the former Yugoslavia. This story depicts just one of hundreds of situations that the UN forces, which included almost two thousand Canadians, were powerless to prevent.

You're at a Canadian United Nations Camp in Bosnia, a twenty-three-year-old lieutenant in command of a thirty-seven-man infantry platoon deployed as part of the UN Protection Force (UNPROFOR). You and your men are all highly trained professionals, armed to the teeth, and ready for anything. At least you think you are. Today your platoon is tasked with escorting a convoy of UN vehicles transporting humanitarian aid for the United Nations High Commission for Refugees (UNHCR).

Mounted in your armoured personnel carriers (APC) you lead the convoy and cover the rear as the convoy makes its way through a small town. You encounter one of the hundreds of road blocks that pop up whenever the UN is moving about. As usual it is manned by militiamen from a local warring faction. You grind to a halt and the civilian UNHCR guy gets out of his vehicle, motions to you to stay mounted, and steps forward to negotiate your passage through the town.

Beyond the checkpoint you and your troops can see the militia guys forcing the townspeople out of their homes and you think, What the fuck is going on? The troops are standing up in the backs of their carriers. They're keen, observant, and like you, they sense something is up and are eager to dismount and sort things out. You watch as two elderly men are pulled from the crowd, shoved against a wall, and shot. It happens so fast that you can't fathom what you have just witnessed. For a second you're shocked. What the fuck? Then your instincts and training kick in and you're ready to deploy your platoon and kick some ass and take names later. You raise your hand to signal to your soldiers to dismount when you hear someone yell, "NO! Stay in your vehicles." The UNHCR civilian yells, "This is not our mandate and you are only here to protect the convoy."

You're dumbfounded, your troops can't believe what is happening. It is as if the civie has not seen what just happened, so you yell, "Did you see what just happened?"

"Yes, and I said stay mounted."

It's like watching a documentary on the History Channel of the liquidation of the Warsaw ghetto or the rail siding at the Auschwitz death camp. The women and children are separated from the men, they're screaming and sobbing, they know what lies ahead and they are all looking towards you and your men, their eyes pleading for help. They are being forced down the road out of town. The militia guys are looking at you, grinning, knowing that you can only use force if you are threatened and required to protect yourselves, so they make sure they do nothing to make you feel threatened...they just smile.

You can't believe a mandate written in the quiet of an office at the UN headquarters in New York City by some bureaucratic civilian means you are now allowed to do exactly nothing. The road ahead opens and the convoy moves off. You pass the two dead men lying in a pool of blood. You need to do something! screams in your head. Your men are still looking towards you, disgusted, they cannot believe what is happening and that you have allowed it to happen.

The convoy quickly catches up to the crowd. They are being forced down the main road and the head of the column has turned down a side road in the direction of a forest. Now the townspeople glare at you as you drive past. You force yourself to look into their eyes. You want to remember, you want to feel guilty, punished for the rest of your life for doing nothing.

The images do not end there. The sounds will also become a trigger for that day because even though you are a few kilometres away, you can hear the gunfire. Remember, you're a caring and intelligent soldier from Canada, you know what is going on in the woods behind you. In your mind you have already formulated an excuse, albeit a hollow one, to justify why you didn't help. We were not allowed to help! You keep telling yourself. Yes, yes, yes, you weren't allowed to help.

Two days later, with the memory of the village still fresh in your mind, you receive orders to go back to the village and investigate what went on, to count the dead, and recover the bodies. What you witnessed was a war crime. You feel guilty, even complicit, in the deaths of those villagers.

As you turn down the road that leads into the forest, you know what you will find. The elderly are scattered about the woods. It looks as though they were told to run, to give their executioners a bit of sport, because it's harder to hit them on the run. Just good sport in the eyes of the executioners. There are a few bloated bodies caught up in the bush along the riverbank, and when you check a few nearby houses you find a dozen or so villagers burnt to death in the basement of one of the houses. There are no young women or girls amongst the dead; all you find are the elderly, kids, and babies. There are no words that can convey your feelings when you see toddlers and newborn babies with their throats slit or with their skulls crushed by a boot or the butt of a rifle, for the sake of saving a bullet. A search of the ravine farther down the road reveals the fate of the men and boys. You find them with their hands tied behind their backs. They were forced to lie face down, then shot in the back of the head. You know that the women, girls, mothers, and daughters were taken to a rape camp hidden somewhere in the nearby hills. Yes, rape is one of the sordid aspects of warfare. This concept is not new; it has been around for thousands of years. Killing the men and boys and then raping the women demonstrates to the loser that the victors have total control over the vanquished. This brutal treatment of women may be alarming to read about in a textbook, but unbelievable when you've witnessed the victims being marched away to be raped, and in most cases, murdered afterward.

You and your men move through the village. Anger and rage are uncontrollable because what you had imagined is now a reality and you did nothing. We did nothing. The UN did nothing. The fucking world is doing nothing to stop it. Every fibre of your body screams, Why, why, why? They were innocent, they couldn't harm anyone. For several generations they lived in an out-of-the-way village and they were happy. You want to get into your APC, track down any Serb unit you can find, and kill every one of them. Your hard-nosed soldiers wander aimlessly about the scene of slaughter, some sobbing, others in shock. At the time you don't realize that the sights, smells, temperature, cloud formations above, that everything about that day is being seared into your memories.

How often can you do that to a soldier before you injure him? The guilt comes first. It eats away at you, but you bury it along with all of the other crap you experienced.

Then one day it's over, you go home and think you have left it all behind. But the guilt, the inhumanity, and the anger never go away. In your dreams you see their faces. Every time you look at your daughter or wife all you can imagine is what happened to those women at the rape camp in the woods. You start reciting your mantra and tell yourself that you were just following orders, over and over, but that doesn't work because you are an intelligent, caring Canadian soldier. That was the war in the Balkans. Guilt and the belief that there is no God haunts you...but you were just following orders.

CHAPTER 4

"YOU GET USED TO THE SMELL OF DEATH IN RWANDA"

The wounds to soldiers are not always caused by hostile fire, land mines, or accidents. They do not always leave physical scars. The mission in Rwanda was particularly difficult for those deployed there. The human atrocities perpetrated against the civilian population were horrific — witnessing human brutality on this scale has a deep impact on the witness.

When Jerry Deveau arrived in Rwanda the genocide was still winding its way up the valleys to the remote villages that had not been "cleansed" yet. The government forces and the Rwandan Patriotic Army (RPA) were still fighting for control of the country. Jerry could not believe what he was seeing: thousands of slaughtered people lying everywhere. Later he would hear the UN estimate: eight hundred thousand to one million people killed in eight months.

Some had been dead for months, some only a few hours. Jerry and his troops became adept at judging how long the dead had been there by the smell in the area. Very few had had the luxury of being shot; almost all showed evidence of having been hacked to death with machetes or farm implements. In some cases they were herded into a building and hand grenades were thrown in. Anyone trying to escape would be cut down as they fled.

Jerry talked about the day when he and another fellow were tasked with counting the heads strewn over a particular area. He talks as if he had been out counting trees or rocks. The heads no longer represented dead people; they were heads, that's all. They counted approximately eight thousand heads in and around a field that day. At least you know that one head represents one person. With arms or legs it was more difficult. The whole time Jerry talked about doing a "head count" he was so nonchalant that I had to remind myself that these were dead people we were talking about. Regardless of how much you try to see things like heads as numbers, your brain will never let you forget and the details and the memory will come back in 3D living colour when you least expect it, when you are safe at home in the "normal" world. There is always a price to pay.

Death in Rwanda was on an industrial scale and for witnesses like the UN personnel, the enormity of it quickly numbed the soldier's mind. First it is unbelievable and shocking, then it hits you emotionally. At first you become angry, and then when you realize that there is nothing you can do you accept what you see and you try put the images away. The shock and disgust quickly wear off and they all become bodies and you no longer see them as human beings who have died a horrible death. Both the dead and the murders no longer have any conscious impact on you. As the mission goes on and the exposure to the genocide continues, the brain will protect you so that you can get through the horrors day after day. However, the brain will never let you forget and the remembering will come later.

Jerry was in the thick of the massacres—there was no way to avoid it. It would have been easy to stay in the camp where 90 percent of his work was, but Jerry was the only explosive ordnance disposal expert and that qualification sent him out into the killing fields. Whenever the UN was required to occupy a location or investigate an atrocity or a mass grave or a cluster of bodies, they turned to Jerry to clear and make it safe from mines and unexploded ordnance and there was plenty to be dealt with. He was the first person to enter a building or area, checking rooms, tracks, churchyards, hedges, fields, decaying bodies, anywhere there was the potential of hitting an explosive device that could maim or kill.

"I was alone tiptoeing around a building full of putrefying bodies, looking at each one and trying to concentrate on detecting mines and booby traps which could kill in an instant."

The enormity of the genocide could not have been prevented or stopped by the meager UN troops that were there. It would have taken a massive armed intervention ready to fight to prevent or stop the massacre that had spread through Rwanda like brush fire. Regardless, Jerry would bring home with him a deep sense of guilt. Wandering around the countryside exposed Jerry to physical injury also. There was still a war raging in Rwanda and the battles were being pushed closer and closer to the capital of Kigali.

On several occasions Jerry and the driver of his unarmoured 4x4 got caught up in firefights. Many of the fighters had no military training but carried Kalashnikovs with plenty of ammunition. And most of the time they were drunk or stoned. Drunken fifteen-year-olds with guns were more dangerous than the mines and booby traps Jerry was clearing.

He told me of one incident when he was stopped and held up while a firefight raged back and forth across the intersection in front of him. While he sat there listening to the gunfire, with bullets cracking through the air, a very drunken RPA captain asked him to get out of his vehicle. The captain began raving at Jerry and threatened to shoot him with his pistol. As is common with a firefight, it stopped as quickly as it started, and this sudden lull distracted the captain. Realizing that this might be his only opportunity to leave, Jerry and his driver beat a hasty retreat. This was just one of many similar incidents that occurred when he was anywhere near the fighting. However, in this case there were consequences for the RPA captain.

When Jerry returned to the UN compound he happened to bump into the RPA colonel who was the liaison officer at the UN headquarters. Jerry stopped and had a chat with him and he mentioned the firefight and the captain's drunkenness. Jerry then went merrily on his way, giving it no further thought. The next morning, he was getting a coffee at the kitchen when the RPA colonel approached him and told him there wouldn't be a problem with the captain because he was dead. Jerry said, "So he was killed in the firefight?"

"No," the colonel said, "I went out and found him drunk, so I shot him."

"You didn't."

"Yes, he was drunk, disrespectful to you, and to me when I confronted him, so he was not a good soldier, so I shot him." With that the colonel took his coffee and walked away. Jerry stood there dumbfounded. Still, though he was initially stunned, Jerry didn't ponder the outcome much further: this was Rwanda and now there was another body to add to the pile.

The tour was a busy one for Jerry. He was always out clearing sites for the non-governmental agencies (NGOs) that started to arrive as the fighting wound down and the RPA took control of the country. One day, while looking over a piece of ground where a field hospital wanted to expand, he was asked to help one of the Rwandan doctors who was working on a child soldier from the RPA. The kid had stepped on a mine and his leg had to be amputated. The doctor needed help to hold the kid down while he cut away what was left of the leg. They had no equipment to put the kid under; all they could do was give him a couple of shots of local anesthetic then hold him down and cut the leg off, and that is what they did. For Jerry, it was just another memory to be shoved away and dealt with later. After his six months in Rwanda, he returned home, angry and really fucked up.

Jerry was awarded the Meritorious Service Medal, which recognizes a military deed or activity performed in a highly professional manner, according to a very high standard that brings benefit or honour to the Canadian Forces. Jerry makes a point of telling people that the medal he wears also represents the outstanding hard work his sappers (the old name for combat engineers) did to keep the Canadian Contingent safe.

Regardless of the accolades, Jerry decided he need to get out of the army. Getting out occurred after his divorce—the tour had been the straw that had broken the camel's back. Jerry requested a voluntary release in 1997. He found a job and went to work as a roads supervisor for the City of Fredericton.

He worked there for three years before he had had enough of the petty bureaucracy and politics that abounded in a small city council. The city officials were an incredibly arrogant and power hungry bunch, and he realized that he better leave before he went postal. He told me he really liked the fellows that worked for him but that he found the "pencil-necked geeks" at city hall insufferable.

In 2000 he decided to put his explosive ordnance disposal skills to work again and started as a program manager for the International Demining Alliance of Canada (IDAC). He was sent to Kosovo which had just gone through bloody political upheaval in its split from Serbia. There had been a massive NATO intervention and the border between Kosovo and Serbia had been heavily mined by both sides during the conflict. Jerry was in charge of a team made up of several experts from different countries and dozens of locally trained Kosovars who did most of the detection and clearance. Jerry told me his experiences in Kosovo could be a book unto itself.

Jerry did not realize at the time that he had been heading down a well-travelled path that many soldiers with an operational stress injury had gone down before. He had returned from Rwanda angry and bitter, he had left the army, suffered a divorce, and then gone on to fulfill his need for adrenalin by going to Kosovo to clear mines. For him, life at home was tedious and, for want of a better word, boring. He had no idea that he was ill. He felt that the army was the cause of his unrest, that his divorce was inevitable, as was his failed attempt at working as a civilian. He went to Kosovo to find the balance that the black and white world of war zones offered—he had to feed his demons.

When he returned from Kosovo the army called and asked if he would like to rejoin. Jerry leapt at it. In his newfound state of stability he married Brenda, his partner since 1996. Not only had Jerry returned to the army, he had landed a great job at the Land Forces Trials and Evaluation Unit (LFTEU) which provides specialized land force trial expertise.

He and another engineer captain would be responsible for conducting trials and evaluations on military equipment, from T-shirts to mine clearance devices. It was a great job, and his colleagues had all been in the service for over twenty-five years, which made for a very comfortable, focused, and experienced team.

Regardless of his satisfaction at work Jerry was still angry. He could, like many soldiers, keep his shit together for the eight hours at work. But outside of work he had a really difficult time putting up with day-to-day bullshit, and it would invariably trigger his anger.

One incident that told him it was time to get help occurred in the parking lot at the Wal-Mart in Fredericton. He was about to park his car when he was cut off by another fellow. Bang! Jerry's anger trigger was pulled. He parked his car and went over to confront the other driver. The man was still sitting in the driver's seat. He rolled down his window and Jerry told him, "You cut me off."

"Yeah, what are you going to do about it?" the man responded. Jerry punched him in the face and walked away, leaving him sitting in his seat with blood flowing from his nose and mouth.

Still fuming, Jerry walked into the store. He figured the cops would be there any moment and he'd be charged with assault. But the cops never came and as he left the store Jerry saw the fellow still sitting in his car with a handful of blood-soaked Kleenex in his hand. This incident in 2003, combined with several others, forced Jerry to admit that his rucksack was full and he was down on his knees. The memories and experiences had festered for nine years before he finally decided that he needed help.

He saw a doctor who sent him to see a psychiatrist for an assessment. Jerry was diagnosed with chronic moderate to severe PTSD. Knowing that's what was going on, that it actually had a name and could be treated, immediately made a great difference in his mental health. He wasn't going crazy. Within two weeks Jerry started treatment and even though his symptoms had simmered for almost nine years, he started to see progress in a matter of months.

Work and home life got better than he could have imagined. He took up wood carving, travelled, and he bought an RV and camped throughout the summer months. He had not realized that his experiences had had such an impact on his life until he started to work on his recovery. He was getting his life back.

By 2007 the medical category that he was assigned was in direct conflict with the Forces' Universality of Service Policy. Jerry's medical category meant he would no longer be allowed to deploy on an operational tour outside of the country. Jerry knew that his time in the army was coming to an end.

At this time, our program was authorized to fill a second position in Gagetown for an Operational Stress Injury Social Support (OSISS) peer support coordinator (PSC). I had been the lone PSC in Gagetown since 2002, so it fell to me to find candidates for the second position. I approached several fellows about the job opening and a few applied. One of those was Jerry. Interviews took place and Jerry was selected to fill the position. Jerry's new career would be challenging and gratifying. He would be providing peer support to soldiers and veterans suffering with an operational stress injury.

Jerry was hired and, after his training, became the second PSC in New Brunswick as well as the PSC for Prince Edward Island. From the beginning he was busy dealing with peers who were injured in Bosnia and the tide of injured from Afghanistan who had started to come home. The soldiers and veterans who were looking for help came with complex, multilayered problems. Most were having problems at work and at home, and half arrived in a state of crisis. When a soldier or veteran arrives in crisis, it is because they have not tackled their injury when they know something is wrong or when their spouse or friends say something is not right. It is not unlike a physical injury when the doctor tells you that if you had come in when you first sprained you ankle it could have treated it with meds and physiotherapy, but now, a year later, we will have to operate.

The number of attempted suicides was on the rise and for Jerry, it meant visiting a peer at the psych ward and then trying to maintain contact once the peer was released from hospital. The suicides were sad and such a tragic waste of life, but for Jerry it meant moving on to the next peer and trying to intervene before this fellow headed down the road of no return.

Unlike a psychiatrist or psychologist, Jerry had been trained to *not* always be at arm's length but instead, make it personal and make sure his peers *did* become his friends. For Jerry being a peer means he has something in common with them—he has an osi just like them. But having that connection means he is vulnerable to waking up the demons he has tucked away.

The osiss program has never looked at how long a psc could effectively do their job. I managed to last ten years, but my therapist said that I should have stopped at the seven-year mark. After ten years I was burnt out, I no longer cared, I did not want to hear about someone's osi, nor did I want to tackle the military or work with Veterans Affairs anymore. It was time to go, and I went.

After five years, Jerry's mental and physical health were succumbing to the wear and tear of the job. In February 2014 he suffered a minor stroke and was placed on sick leave. The stroke left him in a weak and exhausted state and he knew he was finished with osiss.

I think that Jerry, like the rest of us, knows that the cumulative effect of our dealings with peers, and the frustration with a system that has proven its ineffectiveness in responding to the needs of soldiers and veterans, would come with a cost. However, Jerry soldiered on even though he knew that similar to prolonged exposure to a toxin, exposure to someone else's OSI can eventually cause you to crash and burn.

For an organization that is mandated to support soldiers and veterans suffering with an OSI, OSISS has treated its departing employees like crap. Unlike the military, which has its Depart with Dignity Program, OSISS has demonstrated little or no respect or gratitude for what its employees have contributed to mental health of ill and injured soldiers and veterans. When you eventually burn out and can no longer give, you are quickly forgotten and dumped by the wayside.

CHAPTER 5
TEN YEARS OF DESTRUCTION

I t was my first trip to northern New Brunswick since I had started working with the OSISS program. I had several referrals from Veterans Affairs to get in contact with veterans in the area, and this would be the first of many trips to the small towns along the Acadian Peninsula.

From about the mid-90s, many soldiers were released from the Armed Forces because they had PTSD and did not meet the requirements of Universality of Service Policy for military personnel. Specifically, they were not deemed mentally fit to be deployed outside of Canada. Being deployable meant you were employable and if you weren't deployable then you would not be retained by the military. PTSD had become the kiss of death when it came to your career in the military. The Canadian Forces had released hundreds of soldiers who had come back from the ethnic cleansing fields of Bosnia, Rwanda, and so on with psychological injuries. Added to those who were medically released were those who were undiagnosed. Many couldn't cope with the stress of keeping their shit together anymore and voluntarily got out of the military.

In the late 90s and early 2000s the stigma associated with an OSI was rampant and extreme. There was little or no understanding of OSIs and there was no interest or effort put into educating the Forces about them. In some cases the system worked in reverse and seemed to go out of its way to make life unbearable. Many thought that if they got out of the Forces and moved back home they would be all right.

Roger was one of those who got out and moved home thinking it would be a safe place to sort himself out after being discarded by the Forces because of his PTSD. But being back home in Shippigan didn't feel the way Roger thought it would. He found many things had changed. His friends had gotten married and were raising families, and the lucky few had jobs or had moved out West to work.

It did not take long for me to realize that running away was just the first stage in the pattern of reasoning in many veterans' minds. To them, their move home was the cure. The second stage in their self-remedy was to blame some person, place, or situation for the way they were feeling or dealing with life. The most common excuses I heard were the military, family, where a soldier was posted, and what job they were doing—but the list is endless. The "runaway" strategy convinced you that getting out of the military would make it better, or divorcing your spouse, or moving to somewhere else. Within months of following through the runaway quickly realized that nothing had changed and that the demons they were running from had never left.

Roger had mastered the art of running away and did not realize that the constant upheaval of moving only made his addiction, anger, paranoia, fear, dissociation, and anxiety more acute. He thought all would be fine if he put distance between himself and the army.

We met in the parking lot of the Legion. Even though it was quite cold and windy Roger didn't have a coat on. He wasn't tall, probably five foot six, but he was broad shouldered with a powerful upper body and his arms were covered in a collage of homemade tattoos.

When I introduced myself I had an opportunity to get a good look at him. The first word that came to mind was menacing. I offered him my hand and could not help observing what power and force of character his powerful forearms and his sinewy hands expressed. His nose was flat and he had cauliflower ears — the hall-marks of a scrapper.

It was cold and windy in the parking lot so I was glad when Roger said, "Let's go get something to eat."

Getting something to eat meant going to Dixie Lee Chicken so Roger could get his fix of deep-fried chicken, the three-piece lunch special. Shippigan is a small town with a Superstore, Tim Hortons, Dixie Lee, and a couple of bars.

The bars, he told me, were a place to get loaded on any night of the week and fight, especially after they closed and the patrons poured out onto the main street to watch. Roger's enthusiastic ren-dering of the bar fights led me to believe that this was his routine. He told me, "I had boxed at the Golden Gloves level and had a few pro fights and when I lost interest in boxing I decided train in judo and I earned my black belt in less than two years. After judo I went on to achieve a black belt in Brazilian jiu jitsu, which was my kind of fighting."

We ate and then drove to Roger's place. In the kitchen Roger made coffee and we settled in at the table. I sipped my coffee and deliberately said nothing. I wanted him to talk and he did. He was born in Shippigan in 1962, the middle child in a large family. His siblings all still live in the area. He joined the Forces in 1987 to get away from home and he spent three years in the infantry with the Quebec French-speaking unit, the Royal 22nd Regiment. However, after his initial three-year engagement he missed home and he was persuaded by his older brother to get out, come home, and join his construction business. So in 1990 he did. His brother's busi-ness failed not long after it began and Roger realized that he really missed his life in the army. With no work at home he got back into the Forces in December of that same year.

Roger's abilities as a scrapper were recognized by his battalion and in 1991 and 1992 he was given the freedom to train in several martial arts, all of which were sponsored by the Forces.

After two years Roger had convinced himself that there was a career to be had as a professional boxer. So in December 1992, he requested a voluntarily release and left the Forces to pursue it. He said that after his third fight he ended up in hospital and it took him several weeks to recover. "It was a hell of a lot harder than I ever imagined and after three fights, I was finished."

He told me that he missed the army. The camaraderie and the respect he had as a scrapper meant something to him and he admitted that getting out of the army had been a dumb move. So with his tail between his legs he eventually wandered into the Recruiting Centre in Quebec City and to his amazement he was accepted back for the third time.

When he got back into the Forces, the era of political change had caught up with the military. There were mandatory programs being pushed in an attempt to control and limit the abuse of alcohol, deal with harassment, promote ethics and gender awareness, and provide sensitization training. Canada was promoting a kinder and gentler Canadian Forces that was to be in step with the civilian world. Soldiers like Roger were to no longer tolerated or protected as they used to be.

Roger went on his first operational tour in 1995. His battalion was sent to Bosnia as part of the Canadian Contingent with the United Nations Protection Force (UNPROFOR). He went over as a driver and was kept quite busy motoring around the battalion's area of operations. At that time, Canada had instituted a two beer per man per day policy. From the beginning it was difficult to enforce, mainly because alcohol was sold in the camp canteens and could be easily bought through the back door.

If you weren't into local home brews such as "plum brandy," you could visit the black market town of Kisiljak and get any brand of alcohol and as much beer as you wanted in the dozens of shops that sold anything and everything. The drinking rules were slack mainly because most of the officers and senior NCOs didn't adhere to the policy themselves.

Roger was on a roll and just kept talking, so I sat back and listened as he told me what had occurred and ended with him being sent home (repatriated) from Bosnia in 1995. He didn't dance around the subject but in a matter-of-fact way said, "I was sent home from Bosnia because of family problems. My wife had become involved with another man. When I found out I got really drunk and in the morning I was found passed out between two buildings. I was so drunk they couldn't revive me so I ended up in hospital. The doctor said I had experienced a nervous breakdown fuelled by alcohol and they kept me in the hospital for a few days. When I got out I reported to my company sergeant major (CSM). I had no idea what to expect as stepped into his office, and boom, he lost it and raved that I was weak, no good, couldn't do the job of a soldier and that I had an attitude problem which he was going to sort out. There was a lot more to this than me getting drunk I thought, but what?

"A few weeks later when the unit finally decided to repatriate me, I was told I was being sent home as a disciplinary problem. When I arrived back in Canadian Forces Base Valcartier I was met by the Military Police and I was held in jail until they and the rear party of my unit were convinced that I would not cause a problem. I guess someone had heard me saying that I was going to kick the shit out of the guy who had hooked up with my wife. I had also said that I would deal with my father-in-law who had reported me to the Military Police who made sure they met me at the airport. I was really pissed off when I was confined to barracks [CB, military house arrest] and to add injury to insult, I was required to be escorted everywhere I went.

"Two months later when the unit returned from Bosnia, my CSM tracked me down and got back on my case and never let it go. I was under the microscope and I knew the prick was out to get me. He continually went out of his way to harass me with weekend duties and whatever shit jobs he could find for me. It was as if he wanted me to get so pissed off that I'd lose it and do something like punching the shit out of him, which would get me thrown out of the Forces."

Roger got up and poured some more coffee. He sat back down and clenched his fists. The veins in his forearms and neck bulged. I could tell he was really pissed off. With his jaw clenched and rage in his eyes, he went on to tell me how his CSM brought him into his office and raved at him about being a weak, useless piece of shit who couldn't be trusted to do any job, that it was his attitude that had brought on his problems.

"Fuck, Fred, I was coming to a point where I felt the only way I would feel like a man again was to punch the fucking shit out of the CSM and get thrown out of the army."

Then, two days later, an unexpected miracle was tossed his way: like magic, he was sent to another company and set free from his tormentor. It had been a long day and I still had a long drive back home, so I told Roger that I'd be back up in a couple of weeks and we could talk more. I could see that he was upset I had to go. With no one to drink coffee with he'd probably get pissed and head downtown for the evening brawl.

A couple of weeks after my first visit I drove north to have a longer visit with Roger. I had not met his wife, Lise, on my first visit, but she was there today and Roger introduced me to her and to his young daughter, Jocelyn. Later, Roger said he had told her I was going to try and "right a few wrongs" that had been dumped on their family. I wasn't sure what he meant by righting some wrongs, but I hoped he wasn't promising his wife something I couldn't deliver. I had a chance to talk with her for a few minutes when Roger went to the bathroom. In a whisper she said she was afraid of Roger's violent, angry outbursts when he was drinking. She also said that being drunk was now his daily routine and nightly, as I had suspected, he would head into town pumped up on booze looking for a fight to prove to himself and others that he was still a man to be feared.

We settled in at the kitchen table again with a full coffee pot and Roger started talking where we had left off two weeks before. There was more about the humiliation and the shit jobs, how no one respected him, everyone was an asshole, and the talking quickly turned into a rant. I let him vent for a while, but when I saw an opening I dove in, asking him a simple question: "What do you want and how can I help?" Roger looked stunned he sat there, suddenly at a loss for words. I kept my mouth shut, leaned back in my chair, and looked into the eyes of a man who had never been asked what he wanted. After a long silence he ran his hands over his shaved head and said, "I don't know."

"What would make the anger go away, Roger?"

"I want my pride and dignity back."

"How are you going to do that?"

"I don't know, Fred."

"Do you feel up to telling me what happened on you second tour to Bosnia in 1999 and what led to your release in 2000?"

He cast his eyes down and began to talk. "In August 1999 my unit returned to Bosnia for a six-month tour of duty. I was in a new company and I was employed as driver. The tour was going well until my close friend Sergeant Robert committed suicide. I don't know where I was but when the word of his death got to me I was shattered.

"I got drunk, pissed beyond anything I had done before, and in my drunken state I roamed the camp and eventually found Sergeant Robert's body in the freezer container where the cooks kept the meat. They caught me trying to open the aluminum shipping coffin, drunk, bawling like a baby, and ready to punch the first prick that confronted me. I had passed out by the time they got there so they carried me back to my bunk and I slept it off.

"The next morning one of my buddies came by and told me the csm wanted to see me. I thought, big fuckin' deal, so I headed to his office unshaven, no beret, with myself and my uniform reeking of booze, I didn't give a fuck. I stepped into his office, he doesn't say a thing. He reaches into his desk drawer and pulls out a pistol, slams it down on the desk, and yells, 'If you're so fucking weak and fucked up over Robert's suicide then blow your fucking brains out and join your piece of shit, weak buddy.'

"It went all downhill from there. I was never given a chance to redeem or explain myself nor was I formally charged with drunkenness and insubordination. I was given a bunch of shit jobs and treated like shit and after a couple of weeks they decided to send me home. Why send me home? Punish me and let me go back to work and finish the tour. That would not happen. When I left the camp it was worse than 1996 because now there were no problems at home, I was the problem and was being sent home. Being sent home was the beginning of a series of incidents and treatment by my superiors and peers that effectively labelled me as a malingerer and a liability to my unit, the Royal 22er Regiment.

"On the first company parade after the unit had returned from Bosnia, in front of the whole company, the CSM read out the sick report that said I had to attend mental health appointments. Everyone laughed, even those that I thought were my friends. I felt like shit.

"They eventually got around to charging me for my drunken behaviour in Bosnia. I pled guilty was given a fine and placed on Counselling and Probation (C&P). I knew that my C&P was just a formality dictated by the system as a last ditch attempt to salvage someone's career. I was on C&P for six months and much to their disgust, I had kept my nose clean and should have been deemed salvaged. I wasn't, because the harassment carried on, like being ordered to attend a medals parade where the troops would be presented the NATO service medal for our tour. I was not entitled to one even when the CO got to me, the company commander whispered to him that I did not earn the medal. He looked at me and it plainly obvious that this was just another opportunity for the unit to put me down in front of the CO and my peers.

"Another incident that really pissed me off was when I was ordered to see the CSM and I was told to wait in the hallway outside his office. I remained standing there at attention from 0900 to 1130. People came and went and at 1130 he told me to fuck off and be back at 1300. I returned and was again told to wait outside of his office at attention. I stood there from 1300 to 1600 when the company quartermaster (CQ) dropped by the CSM and he had a great gab about me. They made sure they were loud enough so that I heard them laugh and joke about my mental illness. At 1600 the CSM told me to fuck off and be on parade in the morning. I had been put on display at the Battalion HQ for the day so all could see the weak soldier that they said I was.

"By this time I was dry, attending therapy, and attending AA religiously. I kept telling myself that regardless of the harassment I had no choice but to put up with it if I wanted to stay in the forces."

Roger told me that outside of his unit, especially at the base hospital, he was treated well. "The base surgeon recommended a medical release based on my PTSD. Again the unit overruled his expert advice and all I could do was request a 4C Release which is a voluntary release."

Roger fit the profile of how most soldiers were treated and, like them, he was made to believe that he was a piece of shit. There was no hope of staying in the Forces, so he got out and ran. This was the only choice that many soldiers with an operational stress injury faced back in the 90s. They had had enough, things would be better out of the Forces, so they requested their release and faded into the background of the veteran population.

"I got out of the Forces about a month after I requested. I felt depressed and defeated because this would be the last time I would wear the uniform of a soldier. I just wanted to be a soldier like my dad. Even after all of the bullshit I took, if they would have left me alone I would have stayed in. Several months after my release the medical people in Ottawa changed my release to a 3B Medical Release."

Roger is really fucked up. That is the only way I can describe the state he is in.

We never came to any conclusion as to how he could get back his dignity after being labelled a weak soldier. With my help, he wrote to the Minister of Defence and laid out what had happened to him. The military investigated his claims, but who was going to voluntarily admit to harassing a soldier? They all said that he was treated fairly, and realized that the army was not the place for him so he got out. All the investigation did in the end was destroy any last shred of self-esteem and pride Roger had left.

During one of my visits I sensed that Roger was at his lowest. I feared for his life. He told me that the day before he had been sitting in his basement with his shotgun, ready to blow his brains out. "I was going to do like Sergeant Robert and take the coward's way out." He was crying, messed up on prescription drugs and alcohol, and all I could do was just let him sob. Against all of our policies, I stayed the night. I couldn't trust that he'd be OK if I left. So I sat and talked with him well into the night. He eventually passed out on the couch and a few minutes later, I fell asleep in a chair.

When I woke up the next morning he wasn't on the couch and I thought the worst. I made my way upstairs expecting I don't know what, but there, to my surprise, was Roger.

"Fred, want some breakfast?" There he was looking well rested, washed, shaved, with fresh clothes on, passing me a cup of coffee. I didn't say anything about the evening before. I sensed that Roger felt embarrassed about the state he he'd been in, so I let it lie. We ate and gabbed about this and that and I eventually I said that I would have to get going. A serious look came over his face and he said, "Fred, I'm sorry about last night. I want to apologize."

"No, you don't need to. I was glad that I could be here for you."

He was looking at the floor, and I knew he was embarrassed.

"Roger, can we make a deal that if you feel that way again that you'll call me?"

"Yes, and Fred, can you take my guns and keep them at you place for a while? I don't trust myself with them in the house." He went and got the guns and we wrapped them in a blanket and put them in the trunk of the rental car I was driving. Roger took my hand to shake it and said, "Fred, if you wouldn't have been here I'd be dead today." He swung his arm around my back and gave me a big hug. "Thank you, Fred, thank you."

This would not be the last time that I would hear a veteran say, "If it were not for you I'd be dead." For the longest while I shrugged it off. Yeah, no problem, that's what I'm here for, blah, blah. Then one day it hit me that there is no greater accolade than "You saved my life," and that is what we do in OSISS. We give the injured hope. Hope that they will make it through their trauma and be where we are today, helping others. Still, it takes a lot of thought to *not* shrug it off as just part of the job. We often say that OSI casualties suffer in silence. Well, those who help the sufferers do so in silence as well. No medals, no good work, job well done, just that overpowering realization that someone is alive because you cared.

Over the years dealing with veterans, I have come to classify fellows like Roger as one of the many who, regardless of their mental state, still choose to deny that all is not well between their ears. Some make a token effort of working at their recovery by getting prescriptions filled and dropping in for the occasional visit with a therapist. Sadly, some only attend therapy and keep their prescriptions current out of fear of losing their veterans pension for PTSD. Try as I might, there were some veterans I could not convince that their pensions were safe but they should take their meds and get into therapy for themselves and for their families' sake. Unfortunately, there is no mechanism within Veterans Affairs that compels a veteran to be compliant with their treatment plan.

Over the years, Roger became physically ill. The heavy drinking didn't help. The men in his family have a predisposition for heart problems. Roger's dad died of heart failure in his fifties, as did several of his brothers. Roger had a heart attack in 2006 that put him in hospital and on medication. The doctor said that if he were ten years older and not as fit, he'd be dead. For a while after that crisis he was off the booze and in therapy and it looked like he had turned the corner on taking care of himself.

Then Roger got a call from his sister to tell him that their mother had died. He was shattered. It was a sudden death and he was awash in guilt and anger. His anger fuelled his guilt and paranoia to the point where he would not have anything to do with his family's grieving. In his destructive state he was too embarrassed to let anyone, especially his family, see how hard he was taking his mom's death.

He made some feeble attempts to enter the family circle to grieve with them but it was too late. He was shunned, told to stay away. His family knew that his anger would explode if he was with them and it would come in the form of blaming everyone else for his mom's death.

All that Roger said to me was, "Fuck them, fuck them all, I don't need them fucking assholes." There was no one to grieve with and all he felt was anger. The ultimate insult in the minds of his family members was when he didn't attend the funeral. He told me later that he was ashamed of himself. He came to regret that decision in many ways but as far as he was concerned, the worst part of the death of his mom was that he never had a chance to say goodbye and I love you.

He could not face anyone in the community and he was self-medicating with alcohol. I managed to visit Roger about every three weeks and we spoke on the phone every couple of days. There were times when he would call me in a drunken state either angry about something or guilty about having done something wrong. His anger knew no bounds and if you were stupid enough to make eye contact, your only warning was a "What the fuck are you looking at?" He was in a constant state of paranoia; everything and everyone was his enemy. He couldn't sleep and when he did it was because he had passed out from drinking. His family and most of his friends were afraid of him, and only his hardcore drinking buddies could tolerate his outbursts, mainly because they were too drunk or stoned to care. Roger relished the prospect of being confronted by the police, saying that when it came he would commit suicide "by cop" and "go out in a blaze of glory." There wasn't much I could do or say other than listen to him. But I kept repeating my mantra to him: "Nothing will change unless you stop drinking, get into therapy, and take your meds."

Roger's siblings did not understand what PTSD was and thought it could be sorted out by just getting on with life. We all wish it was that easy. Meanwhile, Roger was on a path of destruction, driving drunk, looking for and instigating fights, hunting out of season, and being in possession of illegal weapons. I always expected that the next phone call I would get would be the one that informed me he was dead or in jail.

Suicide was always a topic whenever I visited or called him. During one visit we were in his "bunker" in the basement he said, "No one cares so why not blow my fucking head off?" and he grabbed his shotgun and put the double barrels under his chin and yelled "Fuck everyone!" I didn't react and maybe I couldn't. If he was going to pull the trigger at that moment there was nothing I could do to stop him.

In that instant my PTSD chain was pulled. I had seen so much death already and suddenly it seemed like one more wouldn't matter. Roger was taking a toll on my mental health, but who was he to turn to when he needed help? I couldn't give up on him. I would be breaking the soldier's code "to never leave a wounded soldier on the battlefield." It sounds cheesy, but it is real and only a soldier can truly understand it.

When he was drinking, Roger's anger and aggression drew him into fights: choking someone out, putting someone down, driving drunk, and mixing booze with his medications. One day he jokingly said to me, "Fred, did you ever notice that there is no warning on pill bottles that say 'take with alcohol'?" On the home front Lise and Jocelyn were worn out. They could do no more and they had come to fear him. Lise once told me she thought that maybe he would be "better off dead or put him in jail." She knew that no one could help him until he wanted help.

I would like to be able to say Roger got help and that they lived happily ever after.

Not long after renovating the house they had bought in Shippigan, Roger and Lise placed it on the market and took another retreat to Quebec City. When Roger called and told me, I was shocked, but in a way not surprised. He said he was doing it for Jocelyn. I wanted to scream at him. I felt so fucking frustrated, but telling him to man up would only cut me out of his life. As difficult as his situation was, I wanted to be there for him if he needed me. I think he realized that I was angry and for the first time he ended the conversation. "I've got to go, Fred. I'll call you next week."

The roller-coaster ride from hell was on again. After not hearing from Roger for eight months, he called and told me he was back in Shippigan again with his family. A month or so after his return, I headed north for a visit.

Roger met me with open arms, as if it had been years and not months since we'd last seen one another. We went down to the basement where Roger had set up his bunker. He offered me a coffee and we got comfortable, and then he began telling me why they were back. It all boiled down to the same excuses: the city was too busy, his in-laws were out to get him, everyone was looking at him, and people asked questions. His paranoia, anxiety, and anger were at an all-time high and had followed him to his new home just outside of Shippigan. I felt angry and frustrated. I said, "You're still not doing anything to get healthier and you're wallowing in anger and self-pity, which is a toxic." He blew me off saying, "Yeah, yeah, get off the booze, take your meds, and get into therapy." I lied and said I had to connect with a guy in Miramichi and left.

I would not see Roger for several months. During those months he called me several times, always drunk. A couple of times he called and was afraid that he had really hurt someone in a bar fight and he was just waiting for the cops to arrive. They never came. I don't know if that was a good or bad thing. I had lost any sense of what was normal when it came to Roger.

I was not surprised when he fell off my radar again, this time for several months. Then, out of the blue, he called me. After several years of hearing me preach to him that his life would not change until he was off the booze, in therapy, and on his meds, Roger was telling me that he had finally bought into two thirds of the plan and was waiting for a referral to a therapist.

Then came another crisis. Roger called to tell me that Jocelyn, now seventeen, had attempted suicide. I realized immediately that any progress Lise and Roger had made towards recovery had just disappeared in an instant. Roger shouldered all of the blame, saying it was his fault because of the way he had behaved in the past, his drunkenness, anger, and depression. It didn't matter when they found out that Jocelyn's desperation was the result of bullying at the hands of a dozen or so girls at her school. Roger blamed himself and there were plenty of reasons why he could. He had often said he was not a good father or husband—here was the proof. He started talking to me about suicide again. Now more than ever he felt that Lise and Jocelyn would definitely be better off if he were dead.

I visited Roger several times during the summer. In the fall and winter, the visits fell off and I only managed to get to Shippigan a couple of times. It seemed like the crisis with Jocelyn had forced Roger to get his shit together. Lise was seeing some improvement: he was still dry and on his meds, and now he was in therapy.

But I knew that it was too good to believe. During one of our phone calls he told me they were moving back to Quebec City again. Fuck, fuck, I thought as he tried to make it sound like this would again be a good thing for his family. Lise would be close to her parents and Jocelyn could attend a community college.

That was the last time I spoke with the fellow who had once called me his brother. I expected another call, but none came. In the summer of 2012 I found out that Roger was alone, that Lise and Jocelyn had left him and that he was living in the bush in northern

New Brunswick. The law had also finally caught up with him and he would be returning to Quebec City to face assault charges in July. As the old blues tune goes, "If I didn't have bad luck I'd have no luck at all."

I had been involved with Roger for almost ten years and during those years I saw everything imaginable that could happen to someone with an OSI. It continues to be frustrating because deep down, there is the real Roger, a big-hearted man who would give you the shirt off his back. But by not coming to grips with his OSI he is crippling himself and hurting everyone around him. I hope that someday he will find some peace and balance in his life—if anyone deserves it, he sure does.

CHAPTER 6

ATTITUDES TOWARDS PTSD IN THE CANADIAN ARMED FORCES

n February 2002, the Canadian Forces ombudsman, André Marin, released a special report called *The Systemic Treatment of Canadian Forces Members with Operational Stress Injuries (OSIS)*.

In 2003 Marin published a follow-up report for the Department of National Defence and the Canadian Forces as he said he would. In 2004, the ombudsman's office conducted an investigation into the attitudes of uniformed members of the CF towards those members who were suffering PTSD. What follows are some of the interviews conducted at that time.

Soldiers do not mince words. When asked what he would do if he was diagnosed with PTSD, one soldier replied, "To be quite honest, I would rather tell my peer group that I got the dose at a whorehouse than PTSD."

A SENIOR MEDICAL OFFICER

"I still think there is a stigma attached to the concept of stress-related injuries and mental illness in general, both in the civilian world, as well as the military...As has been reported often, it is okay to have a broken arm, but it is not okay to have a broken head.

"I have done considerable research on military-related PTSD and in my view, the most important single factor for recovery is the amount of positive support the member receives from his peers and unit. The greater the support is, [the] more likely the number of people who will be able to return to that work environment will be. Without it, it won't happen. What the CF is not doing is closing ranks around their fellow members to provide tangible support, both for the member and for the family. The day I admitted to suffering from PTSD, I was expecting support from the CF but that support wasn't there."

A SENIOR OFFICER DIAGNOSED WITH PTSD

"We are abandoning people, instead of banding together as a regiment should, because we are afraid of weakness. The CF should introduce a total person concept and accept that people have weaknesses. We need to deal with PTSD as a military family. We have to get back to the family aspect of the CF."

The stigma also affects family members in the close quarters in which many military families live. Several spouses told investigators they were ostracized once their spouse's condition became known. One military wife, herself from a military family, said, "It's just ugly, downright ugly, and the worst of it is how we're treated as human beings. We lost all our friends, military and civilian. The one military family we were really, really close with...[the military spouse] found out my husband had PTSD and that friendship terminated."

A SENIOR NON-COMMISSIONED MEMBER

"Basically I kept my mouth shut about it within the unit...Why? To avoid the humiliation of having PTSD...no one had come forward yet...Because they train you to be a tough guy. As soon as you've got PTSD, it is shown as a sign of weakness."

A SENIOR CF CAREGIVER

"This non-acceptance of PTSD and other stress-related/mental health injuries is not restricted to supervisors. Many peers and subordinates also have a negative attitude towards a member who has any sort of mental health problem.... We're like the general population in that sense, where the perception of an individual changes when it becomes known that the individual has a mental illness. Mental health and stress-related injuries are both misunderstood and treated with suspicion and contempt, those who have one are frequently the object of ridicule. It's as if they...insulate themselves from the members for fear they might be likewise afflicted."

COLONEL KEN SCOTT, DIRECTOR OF MEDICAL POLICY

"The stigma associated with mental illness in the CF reflects attitudes in society in general. People would rather be diagnosed with terminal cancer than with depression as a cause of their symptoms. In our society we split [people with mental illnesses] off. Nobody wants a mental health diagnosis. It is a stigma. It is bad. Medical professionals who treat soldiers on the front lines are not immune to these attitudes [...] I am not going to exclude health care providers. There is probably some stigma in health care workers as well."

A SOLDIER

One soldier told Ombudsman investigators of an occurrence at a medical facility. "When I glanced at a poster on the wall about stress-related illnesses, the medic said, 'Don't look at that, you will get PTSD,' even though the medic knew that I was there to get a prescription for anti-depressants." The soldier remarked, "I didn't think it was much of a joke at the time."

A SENIOR CF CAREGIVER

"My experience is that those with PTSD are frequently treated with disdain and ridicule. Senior officers generally encourage members to get treatment and express that supervisors need to look out for their subordinates. However, every now and again a unit CO will demonstrate an attitude—discrediting of a treatment, disbelief of a diagnosis, dismissing a member's needs as 'milking the system,' or intolerance borne out of ignorance—which actually nurtures the unacceptable attitudes of the middle managers. This makes it difficult for treatment—it's not uncommon for a member to make good progress within our offices only to see the work undone by the unit supervisors."

A CF SOCIAL WORKER

"You asked how soldiers are treated by their peers, by their chain of command, by the military community. I would say that in all cases, it depends on who is the peer, the CO, or the community. I have heard examples where the soldier has been well treated on all fronts but this seems to be the exception. I think peers probably treat the soldier best because in all likelihood they've been there and can empathize best. I see peers protect and defend their own, offering support for each other, but not accessing helping services that are available because there is clearly little trust for resource personnel such as us social workers. I found out that in some cases soldiers were asking on behalf of another soldier in order to safeguard their privacy and confidentiality.

"I have heard service members with PTSD frequently comment on the negative comments they hear from supervisors or from other personnel they don't even know. They feel they are routinely accused of malingering. They are often insulted, accused of being weak, of using the system, and ostracized by the unit. Their condition is frequently the source of amusement for others, who are often in a supervisory position. Others regard these soldiers with disgust and very little compassion. They make fun of the soldier and talk as if having to see a psychiatrist is some sort of wonderful benefit that they are being deprived of, without regard for the terrible suffering endured by our personnel."

A significant number of individuals with PTSD agreed there is a lack of meaningful contact or support from the unit. One remarked that once his condition became known, "I was the person with the bubonic plague. My unit's attitude was 'let's not touch him.'" Another said he was "dropped like a hot potato."

A SENIOR CAREGIVER

"The biggest part [of the healing process] is at the unit level. That support that you have, that's where the difference will be...the big problem is not the treatment, it's the way that they are being treated at the unit level."

While the lack of support is not helpful, disapproving or punishing attitudes are actually harmful. Investigators heard of the chain of command openly humiliating members in front of their peers. Some members with symptoms of PTSD described their unit's treatment of them as "so insensitive and malicious; it amounted to a secondary trauma that made the disorder worse. One member pointed out the irony in the situation: "I was totally mishandled. I was punished by my unit because I have a condition. I had to spend so much time away from [them] recovering to fight the system." Ignorance and the stigma associated with PTSD lead many unit members to treat their colleagues as if PTSD were contagious, a latter-day leprosy.

A SENIOR NON-COMMISSIONED OFFICER

"I was completely ostracized by the battalion...because most of them were afraid to have anything to do with us...I remember a guy came up to me going, 'You know...I don't want to say this, but I can't be caught talking to you.'"

He continued: "If I went into the Warrant Officers and Sergeants' Mess I would probably be asked to leave. In fact, I know that if the Regimental Sergeant Major (RSM) was in there now, or any of the Sergeant Majors, they would ask me to leave. When I was coming back from treatment for PTSD, there was a Sergeant Major...sitting right there, right across from me. I looked right at him. He looked away...These were all people I used to work with. I think about it every day. It used to make me extremely angry. Now I have a calmer reaction to it."

In many cases reported to the Ombudsman's office, the units appear to have effectively abdicated their responsibilities for those with PTSD. Some soldiers expressed a sense of abandonment and resentment for not being recognized for their contributions. One infantry soldier with nearly ten years of service stated:

"Most people, even the officers over in the battalion, they don't give a fuck—once you are gone, you are gone, you are expendable. When I left, they forgot about me completely. They treated me like crap. They forgot about me, I was never invited to nothing, so I just gave up."

A CHIEF WARRANT OFFICER

As senior noncommissioned officer with a PTSD diagnosis in his unit, he expressed "others' resentment that members of his unit were coming in and getting very upset because a certain individual with PTSD on sick leave, 'would walk his dog in the morning,' and the CWO's opinion was, "he didn't look ill but seemed to be quite happy. He just didn't appear to be sick. The guys at work would wonder 'what the heck is he doing? He's not sick, look at him go. He's running with his dog.' They perceived PTSD as an excuse to avoid work and exit the military with maximum benefits. As one medical health professional put it, "right now all members see is time off and a big pension."

Similarly, some regarded PTSD as a convenient excuse to avoid punishment for bad behaviour or to gain benefits others were not entitled to. Other CF members expressed concern that "individuals diagnosed with PTSD are just malingering, or deliberately feigning the symptoms of a disease to escape duty."

The ombudsman's investigators often heard the suspicion that CF members with PTSD "are faking it" for personal gain. One junior army officer told them that, "in his view, 75 percent of those diagnosed with PTSD were faking it." However, more than one person pointed out that it would be folly to fake PTSD given the hostility and rejection it creates and the potential that they will be medically released. "Anyone who would fake PTSD must indeed have a very serious mental health problem, given the ostracization, stigma, and hardship those with PTSD encounter."

A SENIOR NON-COMMISSIONED MEMBER

When he raised the subject of PTSD with a captain in his unit, the captain commented, "This is a bunch of bullshit. These guys are assholes. They are out there screwing the system and they have civilian jobs." In another region of the country, a senior NCM with twenty-five years of experience in the medical field said, "Some people do certainly regard it [PTSD] as a way of people getting out of work. Sometimes there is not a lot of compassion for these people."

A PSYCHIATRIST

He explained the negative reaction of many military personnel as a way of distancing themselves from the prospect of PTSD. From a psychiatric point of view, "what they are doing is they find fault with the person in order to distance themselves and say, that would never happen to me. That is basically what is going on."

Apparently, those with more experience in the field or on operations tend to be more understanding of and sympathetic to members with PTSD, since they recognize that it could happen to them. The psychiatrist suggested that "younger, less experienced CF members and those most influenced by the traditional macho image of what constitutes a good soldier tend to be hardest on those with PTSD." It was also suggested that "infantry personnel were intolerant of any injury, including psychological illness, even among their peers."

A MASTER CORPORAL

"In the infantry, the analogy I would use is that it is like running with a wolf pack. It's fine when you are running with the pack. The minute you start bleeding or limping then they are onto you—them being the command, the higher-ups, the NCMs."

The Ombudsman found that in a climate of personnel shortages, there is resentment toward those who cannot carry their full load, particularly if their illness is not physically visible. Accordingly, there is a widespread feeling in the CF that those with stress-related illnesses are "malingering." This attitude increases the feelings of shame for many soldiers with PTSD, who naturally tend to feel guilty for letting the team down. The shortage of personnel at the unit level exacerbates the stigma associated with stress-related injuries, owing to resentment at the increased workload experienced by those who remain in the unit unless replacements are available.

A therapist said, "the hardest thing is to convince guys to come forward. If we can make it as easy as possible for guys to come forward, then they will."

Fear of disclosing symptoms of PTSD is pervasive in the CF. Soldiers are keenly aware of what has happened to colleagues diagnosed with PTSD and most are not encouraged by what they have observed. In fact, Ombudsman's investigators spoke to numerous CF members who indicated that "they had stress-related problems, but hesitated to seek assistance because of their distrust of the system based on how they'd seen others treated."

A SOLDIER

"If I walk up to someone and say, 'I have PTSD,' or 'I think I am really stressed out, I am having a hard time with things,' the next thing you know you are in the office and you are taken away from your parent unit. You are gone to Halifax to the psych ward to be assessed. They are giving you medication. They are talking to you with white jackets on. The next thing that happens is that you are on the way out of the door of the Army. Who feeds your kids? Who pays your rent? Who makes sure your kids go to college? Nobody wants that. They are going to fight like hell to stay in, and they are going to dodge every hospital that comes to them. I will bet you that there are a lot of people right now who are doing exactly like I said...Nobody wants to come forward and say, look, I'm hurting. There are a lot of guys out there hurting and they won't come forward. They are not going to get treated because they won't come forward."

A SENIOR CAREGIVER

On the relationship between prevailing attitudes and the lack of encouragement from the chain of command for members with symptoms of PTSD to seek treatment: "Whether they realize it or not, the message that these leaders send out is a profound deterrent to subordinates identifying a problem and coming forward for help. For example, although social workers, psychologists, and mental health nurses have no authority and do not grant sick leave for stress, we are derided for granting stress leaves used by these people with the same negative connotation as 'politically correct,' with the attendant message that it is a detriment to the CF mission good order, and discipline. The majority of soldiers believe that the CF prefers to release soldiers with medical problems quickly rather than try to help them recover, and that the Universality of Service principle requires they be able to deploy or leave the service."

A SOLDIER

"When I sought help from an Area Social Worker I was told, if I requested stress leave, it would mean the end of my career. When I returned from stress leave, my WO described me as one of the 'sick, lame, and lazy.' Whether intentionally or not, the CF has created an impression of the throw-away soldier, if you are broken you are discarded."

A SENIOR NON-COMMISSIONED MEMBER

"There probably isn't a unit in the Armed Forces right now that has not got one of its own horror stories that the troops can relate to where they have seen one of their peers or their supervisors, be it a senior NCM or an officer or a young troop, that has been raked over the coals because he came forward with PTSD problems. [They] have witnessed that troops being humiliated, cut off, blackballed, whatever you want to call it, and within that unit by that chain of command...[These] troops have seen the humiliation that a friend has gone through within their organization. Be it a friend or not, the fact that they have witnessed him being mocked within their system, you have created an atmosphere of distrust especially when the leadership is saying that this guy should be in a loony-bin. They have seen that so you have created the distrust in the system. Poor leadership has created the distrust."

A SOLDIER

"In my mind a soldiers' reluctance to seek treatment, often for years, for the most part appears to be justified. I can't tell anyone because, first of all, it's shameful. It's a sign of weakness. It wasn't going to be accepted. I knew it wasn't going to be accepted as an illness by any of my colleagues."

A SOLDIER

"He talked about 'inadvertently stepping on the faces of dead children during a rescue operation, confessed he cannot bring himself to admit he has an illness; he wondered maybe I am just a coward?'" explained the Ombudsman's Investigator who spoke to this particular soldier. "His view is not unusual. Many CF members simply cannot conceive they might have a mental illness; members in the combat arms, and especially rifle companies, are especially reluctant to acknowledge that something might be wrong. As one senior NCM told us, 'Nobody fucked with me, and here I was having a mental health problem. Soldiers aren't supposed to have that.'

"Many members who had been diagnosed with PTSD said that after months or years...their symptoms increased in severity, including substance abuse, decreased job performance, and inability to control emotions, particularly anger. Several described suicide attempts. In the majority of cases it was not until a spouse or, sometimes, children, issued an ultimatum did they seek treatment."

A SOLDIER

"Why I went and got help in the first place is that I came home from work and I sat on the step. I had so many of these attacks; I didn't know what was going on. I just sat there and broke down and started crying. My little girl came up to me and she put her arms around me and she said, 'Daddy, it's going to be OK.' I looked at her and I said, I don't care about the army anymore. The military doesn't mean anything to me. I'm going to get help because of this. Because she needs her daddy."

A CORPORAL

"There is a complete loss of faith in the leadership and the medical system; there was a feeling that I share with many others diagnosed with PTSD. You have to understand how fried these guys are...I have talked to people who I know, but everybody is just so fed up with the whole system that they just want to get out of the Army and go home. They don't want anything to do with anybody. Coming forward won't happen because everybody is just scared. They are scared of losing their jobs. They are scared of how they are going to support their families. They are scared about how they are going to adjust back to civilian life now that they have been suffering through PTSD."

The Ombudsman reported that "soldiers are humiliated and abandoned by their regiment. The regimental system is there to help soldiers through war. The whole regimental system is based on support and the family environment for its soldiers going through difficult times. Often, when the soldiers come out of difficult environments, they look to the regimental system, the regimental honour, the Colours with the Battle Honours emblazoned on them, the guys who died for the Colours, the honour and the pride of belonging to a Regiment. Soldiers say, 'OK, we know you're sick. We are going to take care of you.' None of that is there. The sense of regimental family has eroded over time. It seems that everyone is out for himself and to get out with what you can. There is a sense of bitterness, anger, and betrayal among members with PTSD over the way they felt the CF had treated them, particularly among members of regiments in whom the notion of a 'regimental family' that would look after its own through thick and thin had been inculcated."

A FORMER CF PSYCHIATRIST

"It's sort of interesting because I have done a lot of work over the years with people with PTSD. If you asked me who I would take on tour with me, who would I trust to do the job, it would be most of the patients I have dealt with. I know they can do the job. PTSD doesn't keep you necessarily from doing your job as a soldier. Some of these guys are the best soldiers you will ever see. What PTSD does, though, is it exacts such a cost when you come home to your family, to your friends, and [try] to be a Canadian again. That's the problem. I have been a soldier for almost twenty-two years and almost all of my service has been with the army. I have been around a lot of soldiers. There are a lot of people I have respect for. But the people I truly trust are some of the people I have treated, some of the people within the PTSD group, because I know they would do the job. I know they would take care of me. But it would be such a cost when we came back home that I would never ask that from them."

Not much has changed for the soldier with PTSD. Yes, there are more therapists and mental health workers, but the stigma still exists and the fear and perception of being released from the CF is ever present. Over the past twelve years, the CF Ombudsman has issued several reports on the state of mental health in the CAF. The reports continually describe a system that is resistant to change, even as the CF continues to pay lip service to the Ombudsman's findings and recommendations.

The findings of the Ombudsman's reports consistently point to the senior leadership in the CAF and their lack leadership and care for the psychologically wounded. The handling of the report is no different from the way the senior leadership dealt with the thirty-six recommendations in the 2003 CF Ombudsman report on the state of mental health in the CF. A year after he made his recommendations, the Ombudsman released an update on the status of his thirty-six recommendations which found that only eighteen were being worked on. Most reports in the CF have a very short best-before date after which they are shelved and ignored until the next crisis.

In 2015, thirteen years after the Ombudsman's report on mental health in the CAF, that new crisis arose: sexual assault in the CAF. Stories of sexual assaults were given to the media by serving and released members of the CAF. In desperation, the victims were forced to go to the media because little or nothing was being done in response to their claims within the military.

The Chief of the Defence Staff and the Minister of National Defence responded to the bad press by commissioning an independent investigation by a retired Supreme Court judge. The investigation's mandate was to look into the state of the CAF when it came to dealing with sexual assault and claims of sexual harassment by CAF members. The investigators interviewed over 700 members of the CAF and issued their report in May 2015.

The Chief of the Defence Staff (CDF) immediately called a press conference to make sure the party line was given to the media. CDF General Lawson and the senior leadership looked grim on camera and stern statements were made—"this is unacceptable"—and so on. After all the rhetoric subsided, the CDS said that two of the twelve recommendations would be looked into, and that ended the discussion. The media dropped the story after just a few days, and the CAF was glad to see it die—at least in the court of public opinion. When General Lawson retires this summer (2015), he will hand the problem off to his successor and go golfing.

CHAPTER 7
I WANT HELP!

n the spring of 2008 a sergeant approached me for assistance in nailing down access to therapy for his OSI. As I've mentioned before, the biggest challenge for a soldier with an OSI is to take that first step of recognizing that there is a problem. This man's situation astounded me because he knew that something was wrong immediately upon his return from Afghanistan. The usual big step of acknowledging this was not a concern for him. He knew he was ill and that he wanted help. What follows is his own written summary of his attempts to get help upon returning from Afghanistan in August 2007.

NOVEMBER 2007 TO MAY 2008
Mid-November 2007 I attended briefing at base theatre where everyone filled out the blue book. A few days later, I had a meeting with a mental health social worker. Here I was asked and answered questions that were filed in the blue book. At the end of the meeting I was told that I would be doing a follow up meeting with the Medical Officer [MO=Doctor; I have used Dr. A, B, C, and D to protect their identities] who would then get me in to see someone at mental health.

04 Dec 07: medical appointment with MO ref: mental health cancelled due to snowstorm. I called on this day and was told someone would be in touch with me.

13 Dec 07: saw Dr. A on this day explained to him how I felt and what I was thinking. He then put me on medication and told me to book another appointment to see him after the holidays.

8 Jan 08: attended my appointment as scheduled only to find out that Dr. A had been deployed over the holidays and no one had contacted me or changed my appointment. Here I had informed them that I was no longer taking the meds prescribed by Dr. A as they did not agree with my system and I would like to see another Dr. soon.

11 Jan 08: met with Dr. B and explained my case once again. Explained to her about the medication I was on and stopped taking, she prescribes me some medication at this time and told me to make another appointment to see her in a couple of weeks.

21 Jan 08: after given the name of Mr. Fred Doucette I met with him and had a conservation with him.

24 Jan 08: met with Dr. B again had meds changed again. Same day met with Fred Doucette and some psychiatrist from Ottawa who was here to see how soldiers were getting treatment.

31 Jan 08: met with Dr. B again explained how I was feeling she filled out the paperwork to send over to mental health. She then decided to change the dosage of my meds and schedule me another appointment to see her in a week.

04 Feb 08: met with Dr. B again she asked how I was feeling I answered "confused," she said why and I said because you are not a psychiatrist and I don't understand why I am not over there talking to one of them. She then made an appointment with therapist C at the Base Mental Health Clinic.

07 Feb 08: met with therapist C and explained my situation once again. After talking with her she said I needed to see Dr. D the head psychiatrist. I then asked if I have to see Dr. D the head psychiatrist then who are you. She then explained to me that she was a social worker. So here I am back to square one right where I started with a social worker. Now this is really not making any sense to me and I am even more stressed out and confused. But she made an appointment for me to see the Psychiatrist which is what the MO had failed to do.

13 Feb 08: met with Mr. Fred Doucette and talked a while.

18 Feb 08: met with Dr. B again and explained how I was feeling she readjusted my medication and rebooked me.

03 March 08: met with Dr. B she readjusted my medication.

17 March 08: still very tired and not getting much sleep met with Dr. B again and she readjusted my medication.

03 April 08: Met with Dr. D the head psychiatrist, I explained how I had been feeling and what I had been going thru for the past few months he prescribed me some different meds and sent me home for 30 days sick leave.

07 April 08: met with Dr. B informed her that Dr. D had requested 30 days sick leave, she proceeded to place me on temporary category and filled out the 30 day sick leave pass.

24 April 08: met with Dr. D and he has requested I go to Saint John to the sleep clinic. Here we filled out and submitted the paperwork.

29 April 08: met with Dr. B and informed her of the sleep clinic.

08 May 08: met with Dr. D and informed him I would be going to the sleep clinic the next day. He said OK let's wait until your next appointment and see what they have to say from the sleep clinic.

09 May 08: arrived at the sleep clinic had a lengthy discussion about my problems here I was informed that this was not the right avenue and she would be submitting a report to Dr. D.

Between November and May the sergeant had seen four different doctors, had been prescribed a pile of different medications, and attended some twenty-odd medical appointments. He had jumped through all the hoops at the Base Medical Clinic and he still was no further ahead than when he started back in November. If anything, his situation was getting worse.

His treatment was not the exception but the rule at the Base Gagetown Mental Health Clinic. This is what soldiers faced when they looked for help. Among the troops the word spread like wildfire that the mental health clinic was inefficient, mismanaged, and that you should not bother going there if you were looking for help. Sadly, I have no idea how many soldiers decided to avoid the clinic because of the bad reputation it had. They would not take that first big step toward restoring their mental health because they had lost the trust of the system that is supposed to be there for them. In many cases it would take a crisis in their lives to force them through the door of the CF mental health system.

I was naive to think that the top brass and the medical branch of the CAF would start to deal with the stigma of mental illness when faced with the Ombudsman's reports and the attention of the media. Mental health education and awareness within the CF is still nonexistent. What training there is, is usually left to a few briefings presented prior to an operational deployment.

During my years with OSISS it was a firm policy that soldiers would not be forced to attend mandatory training on mental health. We asked why.

A precedent had been set in the 1980s and '90s when soldiers were inundated with mandatory programs such as gender awareness briefings, Standard for Harassment and Racism Prevention (SHARP) training, sensitivity training dealing with visible minorities, and so on. They were all designed to make us kinder and gentler soldiers. This type of mandatory "tick in the box" training had little effect on the attitudes of the soldiers unless there were consequences for failing to follow the new rules.

The CAF approach to harassment training was to take the easy way out. They introduced what was basically a civilian workplace harassment program into a military environment. We received "do and don't do" training and were put through various scenarios that had no bearing on the work situations found in a real military environment, especially in the combat arms (infantry, combat engineers, artillery, and armoured) units. When I think of my thirty-two years as a soldier, I can honestly say I was never harassed. I was yelled at, sworn at—as an individual and as part of a group—but it was never malicious. Christ, my job was to "close with and destroy the enemy"—in other words, kill people. Getting yelled at or motivated to do your job was part of soldiering, and if you didn't like it you shouldn't have joined the army.

But as I write this in 2014, there is still no CF-wide education program on any aspect of mental health. Those of us involved with soldiers and veterans could not understand why something as simple as an education program wasn't coming down from on high.

In 2009 there was an attempt to get the message out, with the launch of the "Be the Difference" campaign. Those of us stumbling along with bits and pieces of a cobbled-together education package hoped that the Chief of the Defence Staff General Natyznczyk would finally make a public statement to the effect that mental health is just as important as physical health. We also hoped that he would announce a mandatory program that would make commanding officers accountable to their chain of command to ensure their troops were brought up to speed on OSIs and the stigma attached to them.

The CDS made a speech that aired for thirty seconds on the evening news. Unfortunately his message was weak and, in our opinion, would change nothing. Posters and brochures were produced, and a touchy-feely video. None of this had any impact in the CAF, nor was there any interest on the part of the media in the mental health of Canada's soldiers. Throughout the CAF you can still find boxes of CDs, posters, and brochures, unopened and unused because it was not even mandatory to put up the posters or make the brochures available or allocate the time required to watch the video.

In a very short time it became evident that the "Be the Difference" campaign had made no difference. The absurd excuse the spin doctors gave was that Michael Jackson had died on the same day as the CDS briefing, and that the media and the public were overwhelmed.

It had been a weak campaign from the beginning. The CDS came across as though he were talking about having regular dental checkups, when what was needed in the CF was a direct order to make mental-health knowledge mandatory, to make it mandatory that all members of the CF, regardless of rank, attend mental health briefings, and within the year, or else heads would roll.

I will admit that the system did make an effort to get the message out. Realizing that no one was listening during the first launch, the program was launched again a few months later. The media walked away from the second launch because it was already old news to them. Once again, there were no conditions attached, no consequences for not complying.

The stigma and the labelling of PTSD as a second-class injury in comparison to a physical injury was really brought home to me on the International Day of Persons with Disabilities at Base Gagetown in 2011. The CF has imported initiatives and programs from the private sector and reworked them to suit their need. Programs like Women in the Workplace, Visible Minorities, Aboriginal Awareness Day, and so on.

In 2011 at Base Gagetown, Persons with Disabilities Day was recognized with a full schedule of briefings, workshops, guest speakers, and speeches by the leadership on the importance of and the contribution made by persons with physical disabilities.

At OSISS we had no idea that a day had been set aside for persons with disabilities. I found out about it in the newspaper a few days later when I read an article describing what had apparently been a very successful event. I read the article several times. There had been absolutely nothing acknowledging persons with mental health disabilities. It just reaffirmed for me the fact that an OSI is considered a secondary injury.

I was angry because here was an opportunity to create a bit of cohesion between physical and psychological injuries, which in most cases, become one and the same. Failing to include personnel with mental-health injuries perpetuated the perception (and perception is reality) that OSIs are not real injuries. The stigma still existed, nothing had changed, and sadly, in some cases, soldiers who internalized the implied message coming out of that event actually regressed in their therapy. It also sent a message to the undiagnosed along the lines of: the system doesn't care, so it's best keep your mouth shut.

After reading the article, I took a few days to cool off before I attempted to bring this obvious oversight to the leadership at Base Gagetown. In my email to the commander of Base Gagetown I said that what I was looking for was a commitment to include mental health as a disability for next year's event. I was not particularly surprised when the commander didn't have the courtesy to reply to my email or phone calls. For me and my peers, the omission of mental health from the day's agenda was a clear indication that for all the progress we thought we had made, awareness was still limited and it was still possible for the issue to be entirely ignored or forgotten.

Several days later I was having a coffee with a friend (and veteran) and when I told him about what had happened, he summed it up by saying, "They just don't get it."

CHAPTER 8
HOPE

W hen the casualties from operations in Afghanistan started to mount, OSISS manager Lieutenant Colonel Grenier identified a gap in the support offered by the program. At that point it covered serving soldiers, veterans, and their families, however, there was no long-term support for the families of the fallen. The trauma of losing a loved one can quickly evolve into PTSD. Initially there is a lot of support for the bereaved, but death is difficult to be around and as support slowly drifts away, you are on your own. We've all been there, offering someone condolences and help if they need it, secretly hoping they don't.

So HOPE, Helping Others by Providing Empathy, was born. Its aim was to provide peer support to those who have lost a loved one in the service. Who better to offer support than someone who has experienced the same loss? On the other hand, HOPE volunteers are able to make something of their own loss by helping others.

Jim Davis was involved with the HOPE program from its beginning. I met Jim at one of his presentations in which he described getting the kind of call that changes your life forever. Jim kindly offered to write the following account of his experiences.

THE MOMENT OF THE CALL

by Jim Davis

On the morning of March 2, 2006, I awoke to the sound of the clock radio. They were broadcasting the news headlines.

I can still hear those words, "Canadian soldier killed in Afghanistan." I can distinctly remember thinking it couldn't possibly be my son Paul, not out of some 2,500 soldiers. Those odds are too great. I did, however, think some family out there was going to receive bad news. I then proceeded to start my day, but for whatever reason, I chose not to listen to the news that morning. I just completely blocked it out.

When Sharon came into the kitchen I didn't say, "A Canadian soldier was killed today," and what is strange is that she also heard the headlines and did the exact same thing. She didn't even mention it.

Then at nine o'clock the sound of the phone ringing changed our lives forever.

I remember thinking, Sharon is talking to Melanie—why would Melanie be calling us so early? It had to be only seven o'clock her time. She was never up this early.

It was at that moment I heard Sharon saying, "Oh please, Mel, please tell me he is all right."

Then it hit me: Paul was in that accident. How could he have been? It's just not possible...Oh please, God, please make it so he is OK...Please, just a broken leg or something minor.

Then, lowering the phone and burying her head in her hands, Sharon began to sob, "Oh no."

I put my hands on her shoulders and asked, "What is it, is he OK?...Tell me he's OK."

I will never forget her words or the look on her face.

She looked up at me and said, "I can't...Paul was killed."

It was as though I was instantly thrown into a new dimension.

I was stunned. I became oblivious to all my surroundings. All I could think about was Paul. What was he doing and what was he thinking? I wanted to reach out and embrace him. I wanted to be there for him.

I want to share with you how I was able to rise above my own personal grief and deal with my pain.

There were three very significant things that happened and set me on the right path to recovery.

The first two occurred on the day Paul was killed.

The street in front of our home was inundated with reporters. I remember sitting in the kitchen with family and friends discussing how to handle this oncoming flood of reporters.

Upon hearing of Paul's death, Derek Wells, an ex-Liberal MP and a good friend, dropped everything and came to my home. I am so appreciative of him doing so because his experience as a politician made me feel more comfortable and at ease with the oncoming flood of media. I can now easily understand why some feel the rush of reporters was an invasion of privacy.

Derek, in a calm, caring way, assured me that the reporters would respect whatever I decided and if I would like, he would speak to them.

Then, all of sudden, out of the lull of silence, was this young voice of wisdom. My twelve-year-old son, Craig, who happened to be attached to my side that day, said, "Dad, you said earlier that you wanted to tell the whole world about Paul. Now is your chance."

Derek invited the reporters into my home and with Sharon, Craig, and my daughter, Laura, at my side, I looked into the eyes of this great nation and I spoke. It was a powerful moment. As I was speaking I could sense the whole country listening. I was proud of my son, he was a good man, and I wanted everyone to know what a good person he was. At the end of the interview I noticed there wasn't a dry eye in the room. Wow! Through the eyes of the reporters I could see that this country of ours, that Paul loved so dearly and gave his life for, actually cared and was appreciative of his sacrifice.

Here I was, warmly greeting everyone, strangers, friends, family, and even reporters as they entered my home. I didn't know what to do...how to behave...all I could think about was that I must maintain my dignity for Paul's sake.

I now know that I was searching for someone, someone to talk to.

My brother, Frank, and Sharon were doing their best to screen my calls. They continued throughout the day to take phone messages.

Then it happened, that second incident that set me on the right path. Sharon whispered into my ear, "Jim, there is a gentleman on the phone who says his son was also killed in Afghanistan. Do you want to talk to him? I think you should."

Without even saying a word, I jumped up and took the phone.

It was Dan Woodfield. His son, Braun, was killed on November 24, 2005, also in a LAV III roll-over.

I will never forget his words. "Mr. Davis, you are now where I was three months ago." Those words were powerful. Here was a father who, like me, lost his son, and still had the strength to call me on the phone and give me his condolences. I now knew I had found the person I was searching for. My whole being was focused on listening to Dan. Here was someone who knew and understood what I was feeling. He sounded so clear and strong on the phone. I now knew I wasn't alone and somehow I would get through this.

I believe it was on the third day that the next incident happened.

A good friend, Father Michael Walsh, who had been our neighbour, was sitting at our kitchen table having a quiet conversation with me.

He being a man of the cloth, I decided I would take this opportunity and let him in on my most inner thoughts. I said to him, "Michael, all I want right now is for Jesus to come through that front door with open arms, embrace me, and tell me that Paul is

OK, but, of course, Michael, I know that can never happen. I know it doesn't work that way, so I don't really expect that."

His response really took me by surprise. It was so simple an answer, so easy and so clear that it made real sense to me and made me think.

"But Jim, Jesus has come to you. I see Him coming to you every day. He comes in the form of all the strangers and friends walking through your front door and all the phone calls and cards you receive."

He was right, and from that moment on I decided that I would continue to welcome strangers into my life. If that is the way God was going to speak to me then I was going to let that happen and welcome His comfort.

I received a phone call from someone in DND sometime in late April asking if I would like to attend a one-day widow's conference in Edmonton. Without hesitation, I jumped at the opportunity.

I have attended a lot of business meetings, workshops, and conferences over the years, but I have never attended one so powerful and intense.

I remember walking into the conference room and noticing there were seven young women and one older gentleman. The women seemed to have already bonded and four of them had already developed friendships, but the gentleman appeared to be very quiet and my first impression of him was that he was studying his surroundings and the whole situation.

For the next twenty-one months that gentleman played a very key role in my life. He showed me that there was light at the end of the tunnel and he led me from the dark side to that light. He didn't do that intentionally, that's just the way things unfolded. How he did that, I would need more chapters of this book to tell you. About all the stories he told me, about all the conversations he and I shared, and about all the phone calls in the middle of the night. And, probably the most significant of all, about how he lived out the last six months of his life. In the twenty-first month of my knowing him he lost his battle with cancer and quietly passed away.

That gentleman was Brian Isfeld.

Twelve years earlier, on June 21, 1994, he had lost his son, Master Corporal Mark Isfeld. Mark was killed in Croatia, while trying to clear a minefield. I remember watching a mini documentary about the death of Mark Isfeld and during the piece his mom made a point that demonstrated the Canadian attitude about soldiers being killed on operations. The death of her son had clearly taken its toll on her, she looked exhausted and angry. Looking straight at the camera she said, "Do you know what the lead item on the national news was on the day Mark was killed? It was about fucking O. J. Simpson trying a glove on at his trial for murder. Mark's death was the eighth item on the Canadian national news."

Six months later, at a workshop in Ottawa, the opportunity arose for me to ask Brian a very important question. Our group had just been given the news that we had lost another four. I wasn't prepared for those words and they hit me hard. I left the room and went outside to cry in private.

Brian came out and while both of us were puffing on our cigarettes, I asked, "Brian, does it ever get any better?"

I looked over at him, saw him deeply inhale, look up at the clouds—I could tell he was in deep thought—and then simply blurt out, "Nope."

I then knew I had to accept that. I knew I must find a way to live with my pain. I must find something constructive and positive out of my son's death. Standing there on the doorstep with Brian, listening to him, made me realize I was in the right place. This is it. This is where I belong.

Lieutenant Colonel Stephane Grenier told us that this group belonged exclusively to us. At that time there were only nine of us. We were to have total say in how it should function and Brian often told me that if anyone should take that control away from us then he was out of the program.

I often reflect back to that day in Ottawa. There we were, all nine of us, sitting around a conference table, listening to each other's stories. That was powerful. I listened to every single word said that day. I cried with each and every story. Not only did I cry, but I felt the loneliness, the pain, the fear, and the guilt that each of the widows were feeling. But, most important of all, we not only shared our grief, we shared laughter.

Something magical happened that day. We were inspired. Inspired to move forward and form a group that would be able to reach out and help others who were suffering the same loss we were.

I think it is important for me to say here that our peer support group does not provide counselling. What we do provide is empathy by listening. We know that those in pain of having lost a loved one are the only ones who can identify with others who have suffered a similar loss.

I have heard and read stories of soldiers coming home from theatre suffering with post-traumatic stress. I think I know what that is. I read Fred's book *Empty Casing* and *Shake Hands with the Devil* by Roméo Dallaire. I have watched documentaries and read countless articles on the subject. I can tell you with confidence that I understand why a soldier can end up suffering from it, but there is one thing that I know for certain and that is, I do not have a clue what it feels like.

That is why I know no one else, other than those who have suffered similar loss, can possibly know what it is like to have a son or daughter killed in the Canadian Armed Forces. That is why when the father of another fallen soldier called me the day Paul died to tell me he knew what I was going through, I knew I had to reach out to help myself and to help others.

CHAPTER 9
PTSD ON DOMESTIC OPERATIONS: SWISSAIR FLIGHT 111

The public and, sadly, the top brass in the Forces, tend to assume that the only way a soldier can be psychologically injured is on operations outside of the country. So when Swissair Flight 111 went down off the coast of Nova Scotia, no one imagined that the crash would be the source of hundreds of cases of PTSD among responders, both Canadian military and civilians.

In the darkness of September 2, 1998, a plane nose-dived into the Atlantic Ocean several kilometres off shore from the picturesque fishing village of Peggys Cove. Local fishers heard the low-flying jet, then instant silence. They raced to their boats and were the first on the scene, vainly searching for survivors. There were none. All 229 passengers and crew on board were dead. By morning it was apparent that the rescue was now a recovery operation. In the days that followed, they searched for parts of the aircraft and for bodies—in most cases pieces of bodies. Even as what had happened began to sink in, none of the fishers realized that they would be the first psychological casualties from the recovery of

Flight 111. During that first day, the local fishers were replaced by the Navy, Coast Guard, Air Force, and Army.

At that time, I was the Second in Command (2IC) of G Company, 2nd Battalion of The Royal Canadian Regiment (RCR), and we had just returned to work from a few weeks of summer leave. The company was increased to about 120 troops for our upcoming NATO tour to Bosnia in 1999, and everyone was settling into their new jobs. Three young lieutenants had just been posted as platoon commanders and were keen to meet their troops. Our company had just taken over the Atlantic Area Immediate Reaction Unit (IRU) duties, which meant it was on eight hours' notice to move anywhere within the Atlantic area.

That morning I was in company stores talking with the company quartermaster (CQ). We had both heard about the crash on the radio as we drove into work. We agreed we were most likely heading to the crash site that day, and when the phone rang we were not surprised to hear that Officer Commanding (OC) G Company Major Bill Pond was being called to Battalion HQ to receive orders from the CO to deploy the company to Peggys Cove.

By 1400 the reconnaissance party, made up of Bill, me, and Company Sergeant Major Bobby Girouard (Bobby would be killed by a suicide bomber in Afghanistan a few years later), were on the road. We discussed possible tasks we might have, such as securing the area or recovering debris from the coastline near the crash site.

We arrived at Peggys Cove and went through an RCMP checkpoint established to keep the media and gawkers at bay. The area HQ was set up in the only restaurant in the village until the RCMP mobile HQ could be set up. The restaurant was buzzing with first responders, police, Army, and Navy divers all trying to find out what they could do. We received our task, which was what we had expected: we were to move downwind of the crash site to hamlet of Blandford and search the rocky beaches for debris and human remains.

We drove to Blandford and had a look at the area and the coastline we would be searching. Then we linked up with the company

at the Tim Hortons in the village of Hubbards about ten kilometres from Peggys Cove. Bill gave orders to the platoon commanders while the troops drank the Tim Hortons dry. The CQ, Warrant
Officer Ernie Hall (who was killed by a drunk driver in 2015, a few
months after he retired with thirty-seven years of exemplary service in the army), headed into Halifax to find accommodation and
rations for 120 soldiers.

We boarded the buses and made the short drive to Blandford.
The troops were quiet and anxious, trying to look indifferent about
the job to come. I knew that deep down they were all wondering
what they would encounter on the beaches.

When we arrived, the first sign that a disaster had occurred just
offshore was the metallic smell of aviation fuel. The pilot, in an
effort to lighten the doomed aircraft, had dumped fuel as he tried
to make it to the Halifax airport. For many of us, the smell of fuel
would become a reminder of the disaster. Thankfully the day was
sunny and warm with a mild breeze blowing onshore as the troops
moved to their respective search areas to begin their grisly task. I
thought about the new platoon commanders who had only been
in the unit for a few days and now their first kick at leadership
involved a task that they had not been trained for.

They headed off and I established the company command post
(CP) with the company medic and signaller, then I went for a walk
about. I chatted up a fellow who lived across the road from where
I had established the CP. He was really distressed about what had
happened the night before. He said he had heard the aircraft as
it passed low over his house, and he smelled the aviation fuel as
it showered down like rain. He hadn't heard the plane crash into
the ocean, but he said that all of a sudden it had gone quiet. He
said he had got up early and heard the news on the radio and put
two and two together. We talked a bit about the last moments of
the aircraft and the horror the passengers must have gone through
before they died. It was all too much to imagine. He also said that
he feared that his young daughters might find something on the

beach where they played. I told him that once we were done our work, it would probably be safe to play on the beach again. The look on his face told me that it would be a while before any of them went to the beach.

About mid-morning, a Royal Canadian Mounted Police (RCMP) constable arrived with a refrigerator truck. The constable was an older fellow who was stationed at a nearby detachment. He told me the obvious: the truck was for human remains. He said not to expect any substantial remains because, based on his experience, human bodies in a crash such as this are shredded as the passengers are thrown through the disintegrating aircraft. He went on to say that what was left would be quickly scavenged by the lobster and crabs which were plentiful in the surrounding waters. It was gruesome and matter of fact, but it all made sense. It reminded me of being in Sarajevo and seeing the effect of artillery shrapnel on the human body—how fragile the body really is.

By midday, the beaches had been swept and the troops had recovered bits of the aircraft, personal effects, and some human remains—bits of flesh already bleached white by the ocean, including one piece that had hair, an ear, and a strip of flesh from the shoulder of one poor person. You might think that finding human remains would leave the strongest impression. But it was the personal effects that wrenched at the hearts of the soldiers. They found pictures of kids, families, and loved ones. There were Pampers diapers and infant toys, which meant there were babies who perished.

The CQ found a place for us to sleep at the Princess Louise Fusiliers Armoury in downtown Halifax, and had made provision for rations from the Base Halifax kitchen. By the end of the day, the troops had swept the area several times and recovered all that the tide had brought in that day. At about 1700 they loaded onto the buses and were looking forward to hot meal and some time to go downtown and unwind after a mentally demanding, stressful day.

I decided that it would be easier for the CP to remain in location for the night. We had plenty of hard rations and it would be just as easy for me to stay there. I asked the medic and signaller if they wanted to go into Halifax, but being older soldiers they said they too preferred to stay at the CP. With the company gone we settled in for the night. Having not eaten since morning, we got our Coleman stove out and heated up our hard rations, basically a meal in a bag, followed by a cup of coffee. The rest of the evening was spent sipping coffee and chatting about our upcoming tour to Bosnia—we all stayed clear of talking about the tragic end of Flight 111. After a shitty night's sleep and several trips to pee (you don't drink coffee, you just rent it), we woke to another sunny day and, hopefully, a move to another task.

Not long after the troops arrived and headed out to sweep the beach again, the media arrived. I was surprised, since I had expected them to find us the day before. During the Oka crisis in Montreal in 1989, I had picked up a few tips for dealing with the media. First and foremost, I had learned to never to trust them: there is no such thing as "off the record." This crew tiptoed around, asking who we were and where we were from. Then the real reason popped up: "Where are the bodies?" I didn't say that what was left of some of them were in the freezer truck. I would have liked to have told them to piss off, but instead I chose to send them on a wild goose chase by directing them to a bay twenty kilometres away.

When Bill arrived, he took me aside and told me that we were to be replaced by some militia soldiers and that G Company would be returning to Base Gagetown that evening. The platoons made quick work of conducting another two sweeps of the beaches and found several bits of the aircraft before they loaded up and headed back to Halifax.

Just after the troops left, two buses pulled in and sixty wide-eyed, young part-time soldiers spilled out. Once their NCOs had sorted them out, I told them to relax and asked for their officers to come with me to the CP so I could bring them up to speed and get them to work. The officers were keen to help even though there was little left for them to do. I played up their part of the mission in sweeping the beaches. I said nothing about the beaches having been swept several times already. I thought it would be wise to brief the troops as a group and to stress the need to focus on their task. I told them to respect and treat everything they found as part of the tragic end of someone's life.

I ended with some inspirational words I had heard Bill say earlier: "This is no job for a soldier but it is a job only a soldier can do." I finished with, "Let's get on with it." I did not realize that there was a CBC Television news crew filming the arrival of the local militia. Later in the week my brother and a few friends said they had seen me briefing the troops on the national news and said I came off as a hard-ass. It turned out the cameras had focused in on me just as I said, "Let's get on with it," and missed the rest of the briefing I had just given.

We packed up and were back in the armoury in Halifax in time for supper. We held a quick debriefing and Bill told the troops that if anyone experienced any problems (psychological implied) they were to seek help. In 1998 mental health in the military was still a subject that everyone tiptoed around. We knew that mental health issues were a consequence of soldiering, but it was a taboo subject. We all felt that if you talked about it you then you must be afflicted with it.

The ride back to Base Gagetown was quiet, and most of us fell asleep once the bus started to move. We arrived back in Gagetown around 3 A.M. and were stood down until midday. After lunch, the CO came by and told the troops that they had done an outstanding job and thanked us.

In the fall, we were paraded before the area commander and he presented the G Company with a commendation for the work we had done at Peggys Cove.

Just before Christmas, I was scheduled for a medical exam, and while the doctor was flipping through my documents he found a letter stating that I had been part of the Flight 111 recovery. I think it was the system warning the medical world: "If this fellow melts down...be aware he was at Peggys Cove." I have no idea if anyone was psychologically injured as a result of our Flight 111 tasking. I know that I, like others, just added Peggys Cove to our bank of "experiences" and figured any psychological impact would run its course.

We got off quite lightly compared to the navy clearance divers, sailors, and medical staff who recovered the wreckage and what human remains they could. The recovery took months and many of the navy personnel involved suffered mental health injuries. The medical staff at the temporary morgue spent months identifying the dead and many would be haunted by what they had experienced.

AFTERMATH

There were some long-term consequences for those involved with the recovery of the aircraft and the remains of the passengers. The CF Ombudsman received a significant number of complaints from military and civilian personnel concerning the recovery operation for Flight 111. The complaints surrounded the mental health of those involved in the recovery. The Ombudsman investigators were dispatched to examine the concerns.

When interviewed by the Ombudsman, the spouse of one of the personnel who worked on the recovery said, "My husband is in the military and eight years ago, he was part of the recovery efforts from the Swissair 111 disaster. I will not go into details about the horrific things he seen. He has been suppressing all his feelings for the past eight years. This past July, we moved to Halifax, Nova Scotia, which is very close to the crash site. He finally told me how he thinks about it all the time, he has flashbacks, he feels guilty for not being able to help anyone, and he just cannot even think about anything else anymore.

"My husband is one of the strongest people I've ever known... always so happy, and fun. Now he is always sad, crying a lot, and feels just hopeless. I've convinced him he needs to talk to someone, and we're awaiting a call on a referral to a counselor. I am trying so hard to help him by just being there and listening when he needs to talk, and just holding his hand when he doesn't want to talk. I feel so helpless."

I have returned to Peggys Cove as a tourist over the past few years and I always make a point of stopping at the memorial that was erected on the rocky shore facing the crash site. It is often visited by the family and friends of those who lost their lives on that dark night. It can be a lonely place on grey days, but when the sun is shining, the sea is calm, and a mild breeze blows onshore, it is a very peaceful place. Rest in Peace.

THE MILITARY POLICE MEMBER
Another example of an OSI originating from service in Canada was told to me by a former military police (MP) member. "Unknown to most, a mandatory autopsy is conducted on every dead soldier returned to Canada from Afghanistan. The body arrives at Canadian Forces Base Trenton, Ontario. It is transported to Toronto along the Highway of Heroes. In Toronto an autopsy is conducted and then the body is released to the military and the family for burial."

He told me that one of the requirements is that "at every autopsy there must be a military police member in attendance." He said that a good friend of his had attended over fifty autopsies. Eventually he could do no more. He had seen enough of the dead and he told his bosses.

I was not surprised when he said the fellow's bosses could not understand what the problem was. He was burnt out, he had no more to give. The trauma of seeing bodies, some of which were only bits and pieces, and the guilt of being safe and sound in Canada, took its toll. He was eventually diagnosed with PTSD and he had never left the country.

CHAPTER 10
TOM HAMILTON WAS KILLED IN AFGHANISTAN

I met Tom in 2006 after he got back from his first tour of duty in Afghanistan. His girlfriend's mother gave me a call and said she and her daughter were concerned that Tom was not doing well since his return. He had been drinking more than normal and only wanted to hang out with his buddies from the tour. "He doesn't seem to care about anything," she said. I told her not to worry, that normally there is a readjustment period soldiers go through when they return from a tour. After a tour like Afghanistan, the majority of them take a few weeks to settle down and get back to living in the real world. However, about 10 to 20 percent will experience greater difficulty adjusting to life at home, and Tom fell into that group.

I gave him a call and from the sound of his voice, I sensed he had been expecting it. I think he agreed to see me not for himself but to satisfy his girlfriend and her mom. Our first meeting was at Tim Hortons near Base Gagetown. This Tim's is always busy especially in the morning. Most people are in and out, but there are those with time to spare who park themselves in their usual seats. All of the Tim's locations in and around the base have a fair number of veterans who drop in for coffee as part of their daily routine. A dozen school bus drivers gather there after they drop kids off at school, and a plainclothes MP (everyone knows he's a cop) sits in his usual seat and pores over his morning paper as if looking for clues to some recent crime.

Then there are the walking grannies who always lay claim to several tables in the corner of the shop. I have learned to avoid sitting in their corner because they *will* ask you to move! Sitting near the silver-haired ladies also means that you have to keep your voice down, not because it annoys them, just the opposite: they love eavesdropping on other customers' conversations.

I have had an office for several years, but I have always made a point of offering to meet soldiers and veterans wherever they feel comfortable, and Tim's has been by far the place of choice. It seems odd that they want to meet in such a public place; I'm sure that most don't realize that my work providing social support means we will be talking about their mental health. You'd think they would want to talk somewhere less public and more personal. I guess in their mind, Tim Hortons is a familiar, comfortable, safe place far removed from the dangers and horrors of where they have served.

I've often wondered what the Tim's staff thinks about my hushed meetings with soldiers. I have a feeling that they and the undercover cop think I am a dope dealer or maybe an insurance salesman. I make a point of choosing a seat so my back is to the wall and I face the entrance. About 90 percent of soldiers and veterans I meet I've never met before, so to ease the anxiety of trying to pick me out of the clientele, I always carry a book and tell them "I'll be the guy with the book." It's like a blind date. I'm always anxious, not so much for myself but for them because it is a big step that they are taking. The first meeting is crucial and I don't want to screw it up and have them think I'm just another part of the system and never hear from them again.

At OSISS our ace in the hole at that first meeting is the fact that we are veterans, we have been diagnosed with an OSI, and we want to help. My expertise comes from the fact that, like the people I'm meeting, I also suffer from the symptoms brought on by the trauma of war. So my simple question to them is, "How can I help?" The help comes in many forms, from passing on information about OSIS to what the OSISS program can do for them. Our unwritten motto is "Listen, assess, and refer." Our job is to be there as a peer to support them as they move through their recovery.

The longer I do this job the easier gets to pick the injured out from the crowd. My approach hasn't changed much over the years: Once the introductions are over with and we gab about this and that, I subtly try to shift the conversation to what is going on in their lives. Almost all of them talk in a hushed tone, sometimes as low as a whisper. To them, what they are telling me is a closely guarded secret, a secret they don't want anyone to know about.

As we talk, we slowly lean closer to each other, our heads almost touching, and I listen and they stumble through their story. I never take notes, both because it detracts from the listening and because notes do not equate trust and privacy. I am listening for clues like "I can't sleep, I've been drinking a lot, I'm angry, I can't stand anyone, I'm lonely, I cry at the least thing, I feel anxious, sometimes I can't breathe..." The list is as varied as the individuals I meet with. Mixed in are the people in their lives: wife, kids, girlfriend, buddies, sergeant major, platoon warrant, doctors, friends, and family. Then there are the places: work, home, jail, court, AWOL, bars. I listen intently, watching their eyes, trying to gauge the intensity of what they are telling me. When they talk about the shit they've seen their eyes narrow, and when the emotions rise their eyes get wider, giving room for the tears to flow. In a man, you can watch his Adam's apple. As he recalls the memories it moves up and down as if he's swallowing an imaginary drink of water. He talks in bursts until the air in his lungs runs out and he gulps air in and swallows deeply like a drowning man.

Next to the eyes, the hands are a guide to fears. Most don't know what to do with their hands and usually end up fidgeting with their coffee cup, watch, or ring. Some rhythmically clench and unclench their hands; you can see the whites of their knuckles — the whiter they are the angrier the words. Their shoulders rise and fall with the intensity of their words, their eyes narrow and their foreheads wrinkle with the stress of opening up. They look as if they are physically in pain, their eyes blink, and they regularly glance left, right, and behind, checking for something as if on patrol. Maybe it's something else. Will someone notice them talking to me and assume that they are mental? Diagnoses by association? Something they all have in common is leg twitching. I call it sewing machine leg, the up and down, sometimes both legs, but mostly just one. The ball of the foot stays on the floor and the heel pumps up and down, up and down, like the beat of a machine gun in an ambush. When they run out of words their shoulders drop, and they fall silent. Even in a busy Tim's, it seems so silent. Both of us are exhausted. Getting the story out and listening to it drains us.

So where is Tom Hamilton? I've been keeping my eyes on the entrance and eventually I scope out a fellow in the line with all the hallmarks of a soldier: average height, short cropped hair, and tattoos covering his arms. Yet other than the obvious soldier signs, he looks like a kid, not a soldier who's just returned from Afghanistan.

He's scanning the patrons and sees my book. Our eyes meet and I nod in recognition. He looks relieved but that look is quickly replaced with nervous realization, that "Fuck, he's here, shit, I don't want to do this" look. I can actually see him tense up as he gets his coffee and joins me at my table. I offer my hand and it's a weak hand that takes mine. He's not used to shaking hands. He asks me if he can get me a coffee. No, I say, I'm fine, I had my fix already.

To take the edge off and relax him a bit, I start talking a bit about myself and give him some basic information about the program. Tom seems to relax a bit, especially when I tell him that everything we discuss is 100 percent confidential. To get him talking, I ask about his tour. He is a bit vague and downplays the tour like most soldiers do. Even the fellows who arrive home healthy and well will avoid talking about the tour and if they do talk, it's in broad terms, nothing specific or detailed. I know from experience that they find it difficult to convey or explain the intensity of what they've been through.

I tell him that Mary Ann and Heather are concerned about some changes they have noticed in him. He quickly goes on the defensive. "I just need some time to settle in." I tell him that it's usually others, especially loved ones, who notice the changes before you recognize them, or better still admit that you have changed. Most times you feel normal, but what they notice is your moods and actions that say you are not.

Tom is not ready to admit that there is anything wrong. "No, all I need is time to settle down." Denial is one of the most common and most difficult obstacles to getting someone to seek professional help. Soldiers just can't believe there could be something mentally wrong with them. In a perfect world they would acknowledge the changes, listen to the signs, and seek help. Life is not perfect, so my job is to point out the facts and hopefully plant a seed of acceptance.

I move on to explaining the symptoms, how you go about getting help, what the therapy is like, and why there may be a requirement to take some kind of medication. Tom cringes at the mention of medication. Most soldiers do. It's the training and the soldier's self-image: to be on medication for anything is a sign of weakness.

Tom is listening but he is not engaging in any way. I know he is here just to satisfy his girlfriend and her mom. I switch my tack and try and get him to relax by chatting him up about who's who in my old rifle company. It's futile. I do most of the talking and he limits his answers to yes, no, and oh yeah. Regardless of his attitude, I know that some of what I am saying about OSIS is being hoisted in. Again I plant the seed, and hopefully it will grow into a desire to get help. Having been a soldier, I know when I've been flogging a dead horse, so I sum up. I give him some brochures on PTSD and war-related illnesses and my business card. "Call me any time, we can have a coffee. Don't bullshit yourself. You know that something is wrong and you can't deal with it on your own."

He gives me a grin, thanks me, shakes my hand. "Take care, keep in touch," I say. He is a naive kid, still not realizing that he's not bulletproof and taking for granted the impact of what he has gone through in the last six months. I watch him as he walks out to his car, not a care in his world and I see me forty years ago, head held high, cocky, filled with the invincibility of youth.

Tom never calls back. I see him here and there.

"Hey, how's it going?"

"Fine."

"OK, take care."

I guess he's found a place for his demons, ignorant of the fact that storing the demons takes up a lot of space on the mental hard drive. Through the military grapevine I find out that Tom and Heather are now married and were quickly joined by a daughter, Annabella. So life seems to have settled down for Tom.

Not so.

I find out that he has not adjusted to his new roles of husband and father. His buddies from the tour are more important than his responsibilities at home. He avoids being part of his family and is always out with the boys. Several months later, I am not surprised when I hear that he and Heather are separated, and not long after that, they are divorced.

Tom returned to Afghanistan in 2007 on his second tour. Like the majority of the soldiers I know, he does not want to be left behind. Many soldiers seek the simplicity of being in the action where there is no grey, just the black and white of survival. There are also new factors that make an operational tour enticing: lucrative new allowances which can amount up to twenty thousand dollars, tax free, for the six months they are away on tour. In the past, operational tours to places like Bosnia offered little extra in allowances. A soldier's pay is like being on a fixed income with no overtime, and rare pay raises based on promotion to a higher rank.

So a tour is a way a soldier can make extra money. If you look at a tour in a financial light, you could say that soldiers are almost mercenary in their motivation to serve overseas.

I have no idea how the 2007 tour goes for Tom. I do know that it is a busy one for the battle group and that a number of troops are killed and many wounded. The next time I meet Tom is in Cyprus at the Third Location Decompression (TLD). TLD is part of the tour and all of those returning home to Canada regardless of rank must spend five days decompressing from the stress of serving in Afghanistan. The location, just outside of the seaside town of Paphos, is ideal. It's August and there is plenty of sun, beaches, and more than enough bars, pubs, and restaurants to satisfy everyone. But it's not just a big party—there is a mandatory mental health component to it. It comes in the form of lectures on mental health and what challenges soldiers will face adjusting to life at home. The formal sessions take up about 10 percent of the time, with the rest free for soldiers to relax and unwind. There are no uniforms, weapons, or parades, just good food, plenty to drink, and an opportunity to swim and relax, sleep, and bleed off the stress. My job as part of the mental health team was to brief on OSIS and the OSISS program. We also made ourselves available to talk and listen, to try to help those that wanted to normalize what they had experienced. In most cases talking with us was all they needed. We would send some to talk with the psychologists or social workers on the TLD staff who would get the paperwork ready for referrals for assessment when the soldier returned home.

The battle group was mostly made up of my old unit and I knew a lot of the troops. I made a habit of checking the incoming flight manifest for fellows I knew, and one of those was Tom. I wanted to touch base with him, see how the tour had gone, and ask him how he was doing. I eventually tracked him down and we talked for a short while about nothing of consequence. He said everything was "OK." I didn't want to infringe on his decompression time so I left it at that.

Operational tours for the past ten years have been dry, and so many of the troops on the first night on TLD tend to get pissed. The TLD staff coined the phrase First Night Syndrome, which of course is followed by First Morning After. The majority of the troops got the dry tour out of their system on the first night and for the remainder of the TLD, they just veg out, relax, and really decompress. However, there is always a small percentage for whom one night is not enough, and they stay pissed all the way through to their fourth night in Paphos, with quick sobering up and a huge hangover for the flight home. Sadly, Tom was part of that minority. I knew all was not well with him because whenever I saw him he was pissed.

During the fall of 2007, our paths crossed here and there, but mostly at Tim's, where he'd acknowledge me with a smile and a nod. It was as if I knew a secret that embarrassed him and he was desperate to keep it from everyone else in his world. My job with OSISS comes with a considerable dose of frustration, but one of the most frustrating things is encountering soldiers who will not admit something is wrong, when I know there is help available for them when/if they do. Tom was one of those non-believers, convincing himself that all was OK and ignoring advice from someone like me who had sought the help which saved my life.

A year later, in November 2008, Tom's unit was tasked to send a rifle company to Afghanistan (137 troops). At that time, the army had a policy that required a soldier to be home for a minimum of one year before they could volunteer or be tasked to return to Afghanistan. Tom had been home for fifteen months and volunteered to go back. He seemed unconcerned about returning to Afghanistan.

Since my son first deployed to Afghanistan, I developed an unhealthy habit of listening to the 6 A.M. news, knowing that if a soldier was killed it would be the lead story. I eventually realized that I would have heard of his death well before it made the news. Regardless, I continued to listen. If there were no casualties, I'd hit the snooze button and catch a few more winks. When there were, I couldn't sleep. I lay there safe and sound, listening to the names, hoping it was not someone I knew. It didn't really matter if I knew them; they were soldiers like me. There was no going back to sleep for the families of the dead. I'd lie there safe and warm and allow that familiar grip of guilt to take hold of me. I knew that some-where in the country someone was facing the worst fear of their life, and was now wrapped in a blanket of agony and pain, strug-gling to understand that their life had changed forever.

I had no idea that Tom had volunteered to fill a vacancy on an upcoming tour and that he was already back in Afghanistan until the morning of December 14, 2008. The lead story on the news was that three more soldiers had been killed in Afghanistan.

In a clear, calm voice the news reader said, "The incident occurred approximately fourteen kilometres west of Kandahar City at about 0900, Kandahar time, on December 13, 2008. Tom was from the 2nd Battalion, the Royal Canadian Regiment from CFB Gagetown, New Brunswick, and served as a member of the Force Protection Company of the Kandahar Provincial Reconstruction Team. Tom, John, and Justin were the 101st, 102nd, 103rd causalities."

Sadly, after six years' involvement in Afghanistan, Canadians were getting used to soldiers dying in that shithole. The news reader could easily have been giving last night's hockey scores instead of announcing the death of a soldier. On the CAF website the deaths were announced in a now-familiar template includ-ing canned regrets from the Prime Minister and the Minister of National Defence. What was really hard for me to take was the statement, "they were killed making a better place for the Afghan people to live." The Forces never mention how many tours the sol-dier had, unless it was their first, and they made no mention that it was Tom's third tour in four years.

Tom was buried before Christmas, but 2nd Battalion, the Royal Canadian Regiment (2 RCR), did not hold the memorial service until after the Christmas holidays were over and everyone was back to work. The 2 RCR building was packed with family and friends of all three soldiers, along with dignitaries and civilians. The majority of the crowd was made up of serving and retired soldiers. There must have been a couple of thousand crammed into the long central hall of the building. Up front were the pictures of the dead, taken before they went over. Troops have dubbed these their "death pictures" because they know that they will only be handed out to the media if they're killed. Most turn on a big smile, thinking, as soldiers have for thousands of years, somebody else will get killed, not me. They imagine their picture will never be used. At the service, the pictures are displayed on the projector screens. There have been so many deaths over the past few years the military has become quite adept at putting on an electronically supported memorial service. The technology allows us to stare at the fallen or maybe they are staring at us saying, "What the fuck happened?"

Usually by the time the memorial service is held, I have come to grips with the fact that they are gone and that I'll never see them again. What I am never prepared for is seeing the widow, children, moms and dads, grandparents, brothers, sisters, aunts, uncles, and all of the relatives that will forever be affected by their loved one's death. It never fails to rip the guts out of me, to see their pain and to listen to the eulogies of young lives that will not be lived. To add to the heavy atmosphere and to push most of us over the edge of sorrow is the piper playing the heart-wrenching notes of "Amazing Grace."

After Tom, John, and Justin's service, the families retired to a room for more privacy and to receive condolences from some of the dignitaries. Because I was shepherding several of the HOPE Bereavement Program members who had come together to attend the memorial service, I joined them there. Being a member of this is unique group of people does not come easily: all of them have lost a loved one in the service of Canada. They are the epitome of human resilience and exemplify the need to help others caught up in the confusion and grief following a death. These amazing people are there to help those who now have to face the same thing.

The atmosphere in the room was tense and awkward. The families sat on sofas and chairs in the middle of the room surrounded by people who had no idea what to say to them. Those who were there to offer their condolences hugged the walls, unsure who would go first. There is no right way to express the sorrow you have for another person's loss. Regardless of what you say it always seems so inadequate when you look into their eyes. It was as if the grief the families were experiencing was contagious. Looking around the room, I felt that something had to be done.

I quickly gathered the bereavement support members together and pointed out who the families were—that was all they needed. I watched them hold the hands of the grieving, look into their eyes, hug and comfort them, and try draw out and take on some of the pain and anguish. I knew that when they whispered to them it was things like, "Things will get better, it takes time, what you are going through is a normal reaction." Any clinician could have said the same, but not with the true understanding of what it is like.

Standing there, nursing a bad cup of coffee, witnessing people's lives changing, I felt that familiar blanket of guilt being thrown over me, the guilt of not being able to serve in Afghanistan. I was staring at these shattered families and I felt helpless and embarrassed that afterwards I would go home and carry on with my comfortable life. I knew my guilt was unfounded, but it came from some deep-rooted part of me that said, "I should be serving and doing my bit." Logically, though, I knew that there was nothing I could have done to make a difference.

I was staring at the scene in front of me, feeding the guilt, taking in everything, letting the emotion rise. Choking back a lump in my throat, my eyes filling with tears, and embarrassed, I turned and found an exit and made my way to a bathroom stall. Standing in that stall, wiping my eyes with toilet paper, I thought, Now

Tom won't have to come to grips with his demons. Rest in peace, brother. *Pro Patria.*

The aftermath of Tom's death was a shit storm of administrative nightmares. The military has a system for notifying a family if something has happened to their loved one, with the worst news being death. The piece of paper that will notify a family is called a Personal Emergency Notification (PEN) form. On the form are the primary and secondary next of kin. There is also a paragraph which authorizes the person who will have access to the soldier's personal information. For the married soldiers it's usually their spouse first, then Mom or Dad second. In my case it was my wife first and my sister because I did not want my parents to hear from a stranger that something had happened to me. These forms are updated on a regular basis and checked to ensure there is a primary and a secondary person listed, but (and this is a big but) the system does not care who a soldier lists. Soldiers come from a cross section of society, which means they also come from all kinds of family situations, blended families, common-law relationships, divorced, and so on. All that the leadership can do is advise the soldier to think carefully before they fill in the form.

The other document that surfaces when a soldier is killed is their will. Every soldier is required to have a will, either written by a lawyer, a do-it-yourself kit, or form 7012-1A, a basic will supplied by the military. Most soldiers' wills are quite straightforward — mainly indicating who is the executor and who is the benefactor. Married soldiers have their spouse as benefactor and the single ones usually have their parents. However, in today's society, relationships can be much more complex and in Tom's case they were unintentionally complicated.

His executor and benefactor was an old girlfriend. Tom's parents, his divorced wife, and his daughter were not mentioned at all. It has to be understood that as with the PEN form, all the military can do is advise the soldier on what to put on their will — in fact, the leadership is not even allowed to see the contents of the will.

The soldier fills it in and then it's witnessed, put in an envelope, and handed over to the clerical staff to be placed in the soldier's personnel file.

In the end it took quite some time and persistent administrative work on the part of Tom's unit for the survivor benefits to be awarded to his four-year-old daughter, Annabella. The survivor benefits are designed to take care of the children of the deceased until they finish school or reach age twenty-five.

Similarly, it took months to sort out the child support that Annabella was receiving because it was being contested by Tom's former girlfriend, who had already benefitted substantially from Toms death. It was difficult to understand why this former girlfriend was being such an asshole. To make matters worse, she wanted Tom to be buried in Edmonton near her, instead of in Nova Scotia where almost all of his family lived. After some negotiation, she agreed to have him buried in her hometown in Nova Scotia, however, it was still over a two-hour drive from his mom and dad's hometown. The whole administrative mess had Tom's unit, National Defence, Veterans Affairs, a private insurance company, and private lawyers trying to piece together a settlement respecting Tom's ill-prepared will. In the end, after an inordinate amount of bullshit was expended, common sense prevailed. For Annabella it meant her future would be secure. Canadians watch the ramp ceremony and the funeral, but have no idea what comes after the mourning is over.

CHAPTER 11

FINDING SHIT AND SAVING LIVES

D ave Camp is a Combat Engineer who searches and finds improvised explosive devices (IEDS), destroys them, and saves lives.
This was Dave's third operational tour. He had served in
the Balkans with the United Nations Protection Force and
the NATO Stabilization Force, and now he was in Afghanistan.
He told me that if you had asked him early in his career where he
would serve, he would never have thought of Croatia, Bosnia, or
Afghanistan. But here he was, a combat engineer sergeant looking
for mines and improvised explosive devices. He summed up his
job as "finding shit and saving lives."

Dave was born in Saint John, New Brunswick, in 1969, and his
family moved to Nova Scotia not long after. Growing up in rural
Nova Scotia, he came to love working outdoors with his hands,
which eventually led him to earning his living in the forest indus-
try. Business in 1989 was good and Dave hired a couple of fellows
to work for him. He had also looked into attending the Maritime
Forest Ranger School to study what he needed to know to earn a

good living in the forest. His plans were all dependent on securing a bank loan to start his business.

When Dave approached the bank, they wanted to give him more money than he needed or even wanted. He tried to reason with the bank but it was useless, and he left frustrated and unsure of what to do.

As the old saying goes, when one door closes another one opens.

On his way out of the bank, Dave passed the Canadian Forces Recruiting Centre. Angry and pissed off, he went in and picked up some information before heading home. That evening after the anger of the day had dissipated, he went through the brochures looking at the various trades the army offered. He kept being drawn back to the combat engineer trade. After a few days of thinking about his future, Dave made his way back to the recruiting centre to see if he could enroll in the army as a combat engineer. The recruiter tried to steer Dave towards the infantry. This seems to have been the norm in 1970; I ended up in the infantry, although I'm glad I did. But Dave stuck with his choice and he was enrolled as a combat engineer.

Once trained, his job would be to ensure that friendly troops could live, move, and fight on the battlefield, while denying the same abilities to enemy troops. All combat arms (infantry, artillery, armoured, and combat engineer) are exposed to extreme environmental conditions for extended periods, by day and by night, without rest or shelter. Working conditions often include risk of bodily injury, and considerable physical and mental exertion is required of them, especially when working in difficult conditions with explosive ordnance.

Dave flourished in the army, especially as an engineer; he loved the work, the challenge, and the teamwork. However, all of his experience, leadership, knowledge, and courage would be tested in Afghanistan. The mission dictates the priorities, and what evolved for the engineers in Afghanistan and became their most dangerous job, was clearing IEDs.

Canada's role in Afghanistan, consisting of operations against the Taliban and other insurgents in southern Afghanistan (Kandahar Province), has resulted in the largest number of fatal casualties for any single Canadian military mission since the Korean War. A total of 157 members of the Canadian Forces died in Afghanistan between February 2002 and October 29, 2011, and of these, 97 were due to IEDS or land mines. The IED has become the most lethal weapon in the limited arsenal of the Taliban and it quickly became their weapon of choice.

In 2009, there were 7,228 IED attacks in Afghanistan, a 120 percent increase over 2008, and a record for the war. Of the 512 foreign soldiers killed in 2009, 448 were killed in action. Of those, 280 were killed by IEDS. In 2010, IED attacks in Afghanistan wounded 3,366 US soldiers, which is nearly 60 percent of the total IED-wounded since the start of the war. Of the 711 foreign soldiers killed in 2010, 630 were killed in action. Of those, 368 were killed by IEDS, which is around 36 percent of the total IED-killed since the start of the war to date. Insurgents planted 14,661 IEDS in 2010, a 62 percent increase over the previous year.

Dave deployed on February 6, 2007 on Rotation (Roto) 7 as an engineer reconnaissance (recce) sergeant in command of a five-man section. They were attached to the Royal Canadian Dragoon armoured Reconnaissance Squadron (Recce Sqn) which included a recce platoon. The role of the Recce Sqn and platoon was to be the eyes of the Canadian Battle Group: they escorted convoys, occupied positions of observation, kept an eye on roads and tracks, and monitored the movement of locals and the Taliban. The majority of their tasks required them to move about their area of operation (AOR) and made them a prime target for IEDs placed by the Taliban or their supporters.

Dave and his section were only in the country for four weeks and had already cleared a fair number of IEDs and mines (left over from the Soviet occupation). Today they were supporting a move by the Recce Sqn over a road that had been previously cleared. The squadron commander was in the lead as they moved into a small village when his vehicle hit a small IED and was disabled. The occupants were all OK and they followed their drill which meant they remained in the vehicle on the assumption that that IED might be a ploy to get them to dismount, making themselves more vulnerable. Dave's section was called forward to clear the route to the disabled vehicle, extract the crew, and allow for the recovery of the vehicle. There was also a kilometre beyond the disabled vehicle that would have to be cleared so the patrol could carry on. Dave knew that the insurgents would allow a patrol to move through a section of road and once they passed they would plant IEDs behind them.

Some commanders consider IEDs not so much a threat as a nuisance, especially when it comes to a deliberate, time-consuming clearance by the engineers. However, that is what the insurgents wanted: to kill NATO soldiers and impose a delay in their operations. This strike fit the bill for a "full speed ahead and damn the torpedoes" attitude by the Recce Sqn commander. In the early years of Canada's mission in Afghanistan, some of the drills and procedures that the units trained for were talked about but not practiced. They learned the hard way; only after casualties from IEDs became the number one killer of troops did the leadership in Ottawa begin to take the threat seriously and train the troops in counter-IED drills.

Dave and his section quickly cleared a safe route to the disabled vehicle and the Quick Reaction Force (QRF) moved in to secure the site. Dave was joined by the civilian dog handler, Shawn, and his explosive-sniffing dog, Alex. Sheldon, another engineer, had also come forward and Dave decided to make the task a teaching/learning experience for him. They set off and quickly discovered that the first IEDs were hidden in the shadows of the huts and mud walls which made them very difficult to detect.

They moved forward, with the dog leading the way when, in a flash of blinding light and a deafening explosion, the dog triggered an IED. Boom, it hits you: the flash of heat, dirt, dust. Then all is extremely silent. Dave is lying on his back, his eardrums busted, his nose bleeding—but he's alive. He sits up but cannot see anything because there is so much dust. As he gets his bearings, he sees Sheldon staggering around, but he doesn't see Shawn. His head is spinning and his balance is all fucked up as he gets to his feet and grabs Sheldon. Then he sees Shawn lying on his back. He's not moving. From where Dave is, Shawn looks like a piece of raw hamburger. The blast has blown the skin off his face and hands, and blinded him. Dave sees that Shawn is in shock and delirious with pain, and he watches as Shawn tries to get his pistol out. He realizes Shawn wants to shoot himself. Dave lunges forward, grabs the weapon, and Shawn starts screaming for Dave to kill him.

By then, the rest of the Dave's section has moved forward with the medic and stretchers. Dave and Sheldon get out of the way so they can get to Shawn. Dave looks at Sheldon, who is in shock, and sees that he's wounded and bleeding from his arms. Sheldon has been hit by bone fragments from the dog.

In no time, Shawn and Sheldon are evacuated by helicopter. Dave should go with them but he refuses. Almost deaf and beginning to feel the effects of the blast, he decides it is his responsibility to finish clearing the route. He knows that it would be wrong for him to give that task to one of his less experienced soldiers and risk the rest of his section's safety.

I have come to know Dave and he is the kind of guy that does not give up. He also did not want to let the insurgents know that their IED would prevent the squadron from patrolling their route—they weren't going to win this one.

Dave carries on and when he looks into a courtyard he sees three locals he spoke to earlier. Now he sees that one of them is grinning. He realizes they are probably the fellows who planted the IED the dog triggered. This is the nature of the insurgents in Afghanistan: one minute they are chatty, the next they are trying to kill you.

Dave does his duty and finishes the route clearance, then makes his way to the medic who takes a look at him. He is sore from the blast and his ears are damaged, but other than the loud ringing sound, he is OK.

Dave credits his lack of serious injury to a habit he has, of always going down on one knee whenever he stops for any amount of time, which he did just seconds before the explosion. Being lower to the ground kept him out of the blast that went up then out. The Recce Squadron would lose two soldiers on the Easter weekend and the engineers would lose one of their own not long after. Sheldon spent over a month recovering from his wounds and Dave knows Shawn was flown to the NATO hospital in Germany, but he never found out how he had fared with his injuries.

Dave's injuries got worse as the tour went on and climaxed once he was home. His neck was severely injured by the blast and required continuous treatment and medication. His ears had been parentally damaged, and he was diagnosed with PTSD. His physical injuries were not going to get better but he could work on his PTSD and get his life back.

In the work I did with OSISS, Dave became the benchmark, the example of how to deal with a mental health injury related to military operations. He linked up with my colleague Jerry Deveau and together they sorted out a plan and what support he'd require while he moved towards getting control of his OSI. Dave's work ethic and the knowledge that he was responsible for his own recovery made for a very productive relationship with his therapist and the peer support he received from Jerry.

The Canadian Forces Universality of Service policy ended Dave's promising military career and his injuries eventually led to his release from the army. His career was gone and he had his doubts as to where to go after the army. The thought of failure rose up in his day to day life, but as Dave told me, "I'm not going to let them [the Taliban] win. I won't lose to those bastards that tried to kill me." Dave continues to move forward like so many who have suffered both physical and mental injuries attributed to their loyal service to the army and to Canada. Today Dave is doing well and makes the best of every day, glad he is still alive.

CHAPTER 12

PTSD AND ITS EFFECT ON FAMILY MEMBERS

S ymptoms of PTSD and other trauma reactions change how a trauma survivor feels and acts. Traumatic experiences that happen to one member of a family can therefore affect everyone else in the family. When trauma reactions are severe and go on for some time without treatment, they can cause major problems.

It's upsetting when someone you care about goes through a terrible ordeal. Trauma symptoms can make a family member hard to get along with or cause him or her to withdraw from the rest of the family. Just as people have different reactions to traumatic experiences, families also react in many different ways when a loved one is traumatized.

SYMPATHY

People feel very sorry that someone they care about has had to suffer through a terrifying experience. Sympathy from family members can have a negative effect, though, if sympathy leads them to "baby" the PTSD sufferer. The trauma survivor can feel as though the family doesn't believe he/she is strong enough to overcome the ordeal.

DEPRESSION

One source of depression for family members can be the traumatic event itself. All traumas involve events where people suddenly find themselves in danger. It can also be very depressing when a traumatic event threatens a person's ideals about the world. Depression is also common among family members when the traumatized person acts in a way that causes feelings of pain or loss. A wife may feel unloved or abandoned, children whose father can't be in crowds may feel hurt that he won't come to see them play sports. When PTSD lasts for a long time, family members can begin to lose hope that their loved one or their family will ever get back to normal.

FEAR AND WORRY

Very often, trauma survivors feel on edge and become preoccupied with trying to stay safe. However, something that helps one person feel safe—like a loaded weapon under the bed—may make another person feel unsafe. Family members can also experience fear when the trauma survivor is angry or aggressive. A husband or wife might worry that his or her traumatized spouse will be injured in a fight or get in trouble with the police at the slightest provocation. A soldier's inability to do their job may cause their family to worry constantly about money and the future. Under the Canadian Armed Forces policy of Universality of Service, the soldier and their family begin to fear their being released from forces.

AVOIDANCE

Family members may want to avoid talking about the trauma or trauma-related problems in the hopes that if they don't talk about the problem, it will go away. Family members may avoid the things that the trauma survivor avoids because they want to spare the survivor further pain, or because they are afraid of his or her reaction.

GUILT AND SHAME

Family members can feel guilt or shame after a traumatic event for a number of reasons. A family member may feel responsible for the trauma survivor's happiness or general well-being. A family member may learn about post-traumatic stress disorder and realize that this is the source of their family problems. The family member may then feel guilty that he or she was unsupportive prior to learning about PTSD.

ANGER

Anger is a very common problem in families that have survived a trauma. Family members may feel that the survivor should just forget about it and get on with life. They may be angry when their loved one continues to dwell on the trauma.

NEGATIVE FEELINGS

Sometimes family members have surprisingly negative feelings about the traumatized family member. They may believe the trauma survivor no longer exhibits the qualities that they once loved and admired in them.

DRUG AND ALCOHOL ABUSE

Family members may try to escape from bad feelings by using drugs or drinking. A child or spouse may spend time drinking with friends to avoid having to go home and face an angry parent or spouse.

SLEEP PROBLEMS

When the trauma survivor stays up late to avoid going to sleep, can't get to sleep, tosses and turns, or has nightmares, it is also difficult for family members to sleep well. Often family members are also unable to sleep well because they are depressed or they are worried about the survivor.

HEALTH PROBLEMS

Bad habits such as drinking, smoking, and not exercising, may worsen as a result of coping with a loved one's trauma responses. When family members constantly feel anxious, worried, angry, or depressed, they are more likely to develop stomach problems, bowel problems, headaches, muscle pain, and other health issues.

FAMILY VIOLENCE

Family violence can be one of the most destructive aspects of a soldier returning from an operational tour. For the soldier with the OSI all they can think is, I want to go back.

The destruction of the family unit can happen quickly, especially if there were family problems before the soldier deployed. However, in most families where a soldier is not coping well or readjusting to family life, the soldier will reach a point where the spouse will give an ultimatum: "Get help or I am leaving." It is extremely difficult for the spouse and children to tell themselves they have done nothing wrong, because the anger is directed towards them and perception becomes reality. Any attempt to talk about it usually ends up with the soldier being totally frustrated and angry because "they don't understand." In a state of frustration and anger, the soldier shuts them out and only communicates through angry outbursts.

The cycle of "you've changed" hits the anger button and the potential for violence goes from zero to a hundred in seconds. Abuse within the family is not always physical. It can also come in the form of financial, sexual, or mental abuse. Charges included aggravated spousal assault, sexual assault, assault on a child, assault causing bodily harm, assault with a weapon, and uttering threats. When the police are called, the soldier will be removed, in most cases while resisting arrest, or even punching an officer—more chargeable offences. If the ultimatum "you'd better get help because if you don't we are leaving you" does not motivate, the soldier will, in all likelihood, lose their family.

Canadian UN Camp in Cyprus, 1973. Me as a private on my first overseas tour. We were there from September 1973 to March 1974. We returned to Canada and a few weeks later, the Turkish army invaded and the country was ravaged by war for several months.

UN Force in Cyprus, July 1986. My rifle section in front of our house, known as at Observation Post (OP) Orchard. Front (L to R): Cpl Young (RIP), MCpl Bomberry, Pte McKinnon, and me; Rear (L to R): Pte Kitching, Pte Paige, Pte Morrison (RIP), Pte Edwards, and Pte Noseworthy. A solid group of soldiers and a pleasure to serve with.

My section at OP Orchard Cyprus, 1986. We lived at this section house for a month at a time.

Cyprus, 1986. Pte Colin Tapp with the 3rd Batallion, Royal Canadian Regiment. We were deployed into the Buffer Zone to be part of the security task force. The US had just bombed Lybia and there were threats of reprisals against the British, who allowed US planes to refuel at the British base.

G Company, 2RCR, July 1996. Road move to Sarajevo, Bosnia, to be part of security for the Balkan Summit.

G Company, 2RCR, maintaining a checkpint in Sarajevo, Bosnia, during the Balkan Summit. This summit was attended by world leaders, but not much came from it other than the photo ops. The locals said the summit was held at the former Olympic stadium, repaired at a cost of $17 million, which would have been better spent on hospitals and housing.

An ambush site in the Zone of Separation, Bosnia, 1996. This Serbian vehicle with four soldiers in it ran into a Bosnian force and was destroyed. Their bones are scattered about the burnt-out vehicle.

Bosnia 1996. The Sanica Valley, with the town of Sanica its centre, was one of the "cleansed" towns the Serbian troops occupied. It originally had a population of about 1,400. When this picture was taken from a platoon position, less than 40 people had returned to their looted and burned homes.

Bosnia, 1996. G Company, 2RCR, platoon: position "Fig Tree Bay" in the Zone of Separation. Once the Serb and Bosnian troops withdrew, the platoon left. This is the place where the visiting Chief of Defence Staff Canadian General John Boyle asked, "Why are there sheep in the trees?"

My last time in Sarajevo, Bosnia, on what had been a Serbian position overlooking the city. One old Serb said, "It was like shooting fish in a barrel." The siege of Sarajevo lasted from 1992 to 1995.

Sarajevo Airport, 1996, my sixth tour and my last. I'm waiting to see if I can catch a UN flight to Zagreb, Croatia, and some R&R. In the background, in the suits, is the lead US negotiating team. Richard Hollbrooke, special envoy, managed to get the leaders of Croatia, Bosnia, and Serbia to Dayton, Ohio, to negotiate an end to the war.

March 1999. Warrant Officer Bob Wiseman, United Nations Protection Force, Croatia, just back from a long patrol with several incidents.

Bosnia, 1999. G Company, 2nd Battalion, the Royal Canadian Regiment. Company Quarter Master staff delivering communication for rifle range. (L to R) Warrant Officer Hall, MCpl Parsons, and Cpl Curtis. Warrant Officer Hall retired in 2014 and was killed in Pembroke, Ontario, after a hockey game when he was struck by a car. The Ontario Provincial Police have since charged a thirty-eight-year-old man with dangerous operation of a vehicle causing bodily harm.

Ralph and Jenveve Beek. Their grandson Corey was killed in Afghanistan in 2009.

Sadly the majority of family violence goes unreported or is handled through alternative measures and departmental discretion. It makes you wonder if early intervention could have worked at CFB Shilo in Manitoba, where a soldier was arrested for aggravated spousal assault with a weapon, sexual assault, and three counts of uttering threats. Or in Oromocto, New Brunswick, where a soldier was charged for assaulting his common-law spouse at their home. That same month, military police at CFB Borden arrested a soldier who was later charged with assault. In cases when the authorities are involved, their efforts can be thwarted when the soldier is posted and moves out of their jurisdiction. At their new posting, the family has to try and get a new physician, social worker, therapist (for the soldier), a new school for the kids, and so on. Sadly in most cases the soldier goes unaccompanied and the family breaks apart, inevitably leading to divorce.

Early diagnosis and therapy is the key to stabilizing a family unit. But, and this is a big but, until the stigma associated with a psychological injury is neutralized through education, families will suffer and soldiers will not seek help without fear of losing their jobs.

Over my years in the military and with OSISS, I have been touched by the unexpected death of soldiers I served with or have known personally. Afghanistan has brought that shock and grief into the living rooms of all Canadians. We hear it on the morning news, while having a coffee, or driving to work. But most of us don't or can't imagine the scene unfolding in the home of that dead soldier.

Someone said goodbye to them when they left the safety of home, thinking, I hope this is not my last goodbye. Then they put that black thought to rest with, It won't happen to him, it will be someone else. The thought that departs with the soldier is more than likely, I hope I see them again...Not to worry, it will the other guy.

These thoughts are coping mechanisms that kick in to reduce the thoughts of loss to a reasonable level that allows us to get through the day to day. Regardless, the families and friends of soldiers know there is nothing they can think that will guarantee a safe return.

There are an extremely small number of professions in which being killed on the job is a genuine risk. Firefighters, police officers, and soldiers easily come to mind. They all have very little control of what events may occur that in the course of their workday. Even within this small group, soldiers stand out because once they arrive in theatre, everything is focused on killing them. That last goodbye will have to sustain the soldier and his loved ones for several months. Then there are those goodbyes that become last goodbyes.

When word reaches home it shatters all that was normal. I experienced being with a family during such a loss and it was sobering and gut-wrenching. It was only recently that the world of psychology recognized the effect on a family after such a loss. The diagnostic bible for psychological illness is *The Diagnostic and Statistical Manual of Mental Disorders* (DSM), updated four times since it was first published. One of the significant changes to the latest edition, DSM-5, is that it now recognizes the symptoms of PTSD within a person who has experienced the tragic loss of someone, especially a family member. Like dropping a stone into a pond, a tragic death sends out a ripple, and those closer to the drop may be detrimentally affected.

This is what happened to the Beek family in 2009 when their grandson Corey was killed in Afghanistan.

It was a beautiful spring day and as the snow banks melted and shrank into the ditch, I could hear the meltwater flowing. I was out enjoying a peaceful walk, trying to organize my muddled thoughts of the past twenty-four hours.

The day before I had received a call from my good friend Bill Pond who asked me if I had heard the details of the last four Canadian casualties in Afghanistan. I said no, that the military had not announced the details yet. My mind raced to imagine my connection to them and what Bill knew. He told me that one of the casualties, Trooper Corey Hayes of the Royal Canadian Dragoons, was the son of Bert and Donna Beek, and the grandson of Ralph and Jenveve Beek. Fuck, fuck, I thought. This will rip the guts out of the Beek clan.

Later that night I called Ralph and offered my condolences. I asked if he would mind if Jerry and I dropped by to visit the next day. I sensed that the reality of what had happened had not sunk in yet, but Ralph said yes. Ralph and I go back thirty-seven years, and I always felt Ralph was one of those stalwart soldiers who made up the backbone of the infantry. Ralph was a really nice guy with a big heart.

The next morning, Jerry and I went to pay our respects to the Beek family. When we arrived, Ralph was in the driveway dressed in sweatpants, rubber boots, and a red checkered hunter's shirt. He was raking gravel and from the look of it he'd been at it for some time. I knew that Ralph could not just sit inside; he had to be doing something. I also understood that in times like this most people want to keep busy because it occupies the mind and masks the pain and heartache that is ripping you apart.

As we got out of the car his face lit up at the sight of familiar faces. "Hi, Ralph. Sorry for your loss." I put my hand out and shook his large, calloused one, and found that his normally strong grip had turned weak. It was as if the pain of his grief had sapped the physical strength out of him. As he shook Jerry's hand, I could see the tears welling up in his already bloodshot eyes. "Terrible, terrible," were the only words he could get out. We stood in silence; not an awkward silence, for we had all been in this situation before, but I knew that sometimes saying nothing was the right thing to do. I looked over Ralph's shoulder into his garage. Like the driveway it had been swept clean.

"Terrible, terrible," he said again as he pulled a well-used Kleenex from his pocket and daubed his eyes and blew his nose. Jerry and I in unison said, "Yes, terrible, terrible. You just never know when your time is up." It's a statement that I've said and heard over the years, something we say whenever we try to come to grips with the loss of someone who has died well before their time.

We stood in the driveway and spoke in muted voices about Corey and the IED that had killed him and his mate. We talked about Afghanistan, Bosnia, Cyprus, Pakistan, and Kosovo, where we had served and where these murderous devices were used to kill soldiers and civilians alike. Our words eventually spun us down into silence as we ran out of ways to describe what Corey and many others had experienced.

"How's Jenveve? Is she doing OK?"

"She's a strong woman. Come in say hello and have a cup of tea." He ushered us towards the back door and into the warm spotless kitchen. Their dog, Fluffy (I laughed to myself that Ralph, once upon a time a hard soldier, had a dog named Fluffy), trotted in from the living room and gave us both a good sniff. Finding us uninteresting he retired back to his place on the couch. As the dog went into the living room, Jenveve came out. I hugged her and whispered to her, "Sorry for your loss." The words seemed so inadequate to convey my feelings in letting her know that I understood her pain. The ordeal showed in her eyes, which were bloodshot from lack of sleep and crying. "Tea," she said. Not expecting a response, she made her way to the stove and put the kettle on.

Once the kettle was on and the cups laid out, she joined us at the table as Ralph came out of the living room with a photo of their boys. Four handsome young men stood shoulder to shoulder in front of their home, fit, confident, with full lives ahead of them. He pointed out Corey, the oldest, and his brothers Robert, James (Jamie), and Patrick, mentioned their ages and gave us a little character sketch of each, then he handed the picture to Jenveve who held it close as if embracing them.

Ralph saw the distant look on her face and the tears welled up again as he choked back a sob and said, "Terrible, terrible." He pointed towards the front door. "That's where I first saw Corey. He was two."

Ralph's teary gaze went beyond the door to the memory of that day and you felt he could actually see Corey there. He dug in his pocket for his Kleenex and daubed his tear-filled eyes, yet he had a smile on his face and said, "Good boys...but they were always into something, like the time they emptied a forty-five-gallon drum of Varsol thinking it was water." He laughed.

"Lucky they weren't into matches," I said as we laughed, probably a bit too much, but it felt good and it seemed to clear my head. Still laughing, I glanced at Jenveve quietly sitting at the end of the table, as if in a trance, her eyes staring, not blinking. I knew she was lost in her memories of her grandsons. Looking over the kitchen counter I could see the kettle was boiling away, but I did not have the heart to say anything and pull her out of whatever memory she was locked on to.

Then the phone rang.

It made us jump and it snapped her out of her trance as she quickly got up to answer it. It was someone else offering condolences and asking about the funeral arrangements. As Jenveve hung up she noticed the boiling kettle and lifted it off the burner. "The phone's been ringing all day," Ralph said as he looked at Jenveve. Then he said to no one in particular, "She's so strong." Jenveve went about making us tea served up in large mugs with milk and sugar. She put out a plate of banana bread that a neighbour had brought over. "Just what the doctor ordered," I said as we munched on the banana bread and sipped our almost boiling tea.

The tea reminded me of a story about Ralph in the men's kitchen in Cyprus. I thought that it would make us laugh, so I began to recount it. "Remember that time in Cyprus in '73?" At mealtimes in our kitchen (mess hall in civilian language), Ralph always had a mug of tea after his meal. When he put his plate down on the table he would get a mug of hot water and drop four British Army industrial strength tea bags in it. He would turn his interest to his meal and not until the meal was eaten would he get to work on his tea. Reaching into the boiling tea, he'd fish out the tea bags out with his fingers and squeeze the life out them. Satisfied that the tea was black enough, he'd down it in two or three gulps. "Christ, Ralph," I remember saying, "why bother with the cup? Why don't you just put the tea bags in your mouth and suck on them?" We laughed; even Jenveve could not resist a chuckle.

We sat in silence, savouring the comforting warmth of the tea, but not for long. "Terrible, terrible," Ralph said as if the silence had to be filled. Jerry and I quickly stick-handled the conversation towards this and that before finally settling on a safe subject: the way the government had screwed the veterans and widows with the Agent Orange settlement. The three of us recounted getting sprayed at various times and places in the army training area at Base Gagetown by a chemical designed to kill plants, shrubs, and trees. We knew what had gone on out there for almost thirty years and the fellows who had died from cancer, diabetes, and other conditions that pointed to chemical exposure in the training area. "Jesus Christ," Ralph said and was quickly shushed by Jenveve. "Don't use that name like that in this house." Everyone knew that Jenveve was close to her God and Christ, and I wondered how she felt about him today, faced with this test of her faith. Looking at her sitting there, calm and lost in her thoughts, I sensed that her faith and trust in him would not falter.

Since retiring, Ralph had kept himself busy doing rough plumbing in the neighbourhood. It was nothing fancy, just basic water and waste stuff. He had picked up his skills in Cyprus in '73 and '74 as an assault pioneer. I said, "Cyprus was good," and Ralph agreed. But I had slipped by bringing Cyprus up. We had lost a fellow on that tour and Ralph remembered the death of Corporal

Roach. He told us about going to the airhead (airfield) to say good-bye to him. Many of us had made our way to airhead to pay our last respects to Roach. His body was there in an aluminum shipping coffin awaiting the weekly supply flight that would transport him home for burial. Ralph said that the medics had washed Roach's body and one of them had lain down in the coffin to see if Roach would fit. He remembered how the air movement's fellow would not stay inside the hangar with the dead body. There was no ramp ceremony like they have today for the soldiers killed in Afghanistan and I have no idea how his funeral was handled back in Canada.

I was caught up in the memory of that day in Cyprus but I wasn't sure where Ralph was going with this. Looking at him I noticed the tears welling up and a look of anguish unfolding on his face as he said, "I went up to Roach's coffin and patted it and said, 'Have a good trip home, buddy.'" I fought off my own tears. Ralph blew his nose and said, "In my lifetime I never thought I would have one of my own come home like that." With a sob of anguish he choked out, "Terrible, terrible..." He daubed his cheeks and eyes with a crumpled Kleenex already damp with tears and silence settled over us again. As we sat there I fuelled my grief with thoughts of what it would be like to lose my son, daughter, or grandchild. I could feel the ache and fear rise up in me as I realized this can happen to anyone.

Thankfully Jenveve broke our trance. "I just want Corey home and close by. Until he's home things will not settle down." We talked a bit about what they knew of the funeral details, which were still a bit sketchy. Bert and Donna, Corey's parents, had returned home late from the repatriation ceremony in Trenton and Corey's body was still in Toronto awaiting an autopsy, as was required for all soldiers killed on operations. As is customary, a soldier, a close friend of Corey's, had escorted the body from Afghanistan and would stay with the body until Corey was laid to rest. Jenveve said, "It must be so hard on that soldier to have to deal with something like this at such a young age."

"Bert and Donna are taking care of everything, they seem so strong," Ralph said. I told him that once everything was over and the crowds had drifted away, this would be their time to grieve. Grieving is something you can't avoid. It has to come out it and run its course.

"More tea?" asked Jenveve.

"No thanks, that's fine, we should be going anyway." We thanked Jenveve for her hospitality, gave her a hug, and again offered our condolences. We said we'd see her at the funeral and that if there was anything she needed, just to call.

As Ralph ushered us out onto the back porch, he said, "Come on, I want to show you some fishing lures that I made." We made our way to the garage and I heard Ralph say to himself, "She is so strong." I think that showing emotion was embarrassing for Ralph. It was as if he wanted to be strong like Jenveve. But from experience I knew that fighting your emotions was a losing battle. "Ralph, you're doing the right thing, let it out, it's healthy. Cry, be angry, sad, whatever comes, let it happen, you'll feel better for doing it."

Fighting back tears and daubing his eyes with his Kleenex, Ralph beckoned us to follow him into the garage to a door at the back. He unlocked the door and we entered his sanctuary, the room where Ralph kept his most prized possessions: his fishing gear. He and his son Bert are members of the Bass Fishing Association of New Brunswick. In fact, Bert is now its president. They were both anxious and geared up for the new season. "But the death of Corey may change things," Ralph said. I thought to myself, They will be on the river at the first opportunity and in doing so they'll keep busy. There will be many quiet moments on the river when they will both be lost in their thoughts and memories—all part of the grieving process.

After a while Jerry looked at me and we knew that Ralph was running on his reserves of emotional strength and needed to be alone. "We should be heading, Ralph." It was closing in on suppertime and I know the family would be gathering now that they were all home, save Corey. There would be more friends coming by to offer their condolences and try to see if they could help in any way. I almost sensed that Ralph would prefer to stay in his sanctuary, talking about fishing instead of dealing with his terrible, terrible loss over and over again. But I think Ralph must realized that he had to face the pain of loss and grieve, which is, in an odd way, the right thing to do. I told Ralph that Jerry and I would see him at the visitation and funeral, and promised to drop by once things settled down. As we back out of the driveway Ralph began raking again, staring off into the distance, lost in his memories.

Corey's death placed a lot of stress on the family and it put a divide between his mom and dad, which eventually led to a separation and then divorce. Whenever I meet Ralph, I sense that he has aged and is less the man I once knew. I guess tired would be the word to describe him. I know his big heart is broken.

CHAPTER 13
MY EXPERIENCE WITH PTSD

By the Christmas of 1995, after six months in Sarajevo, I'd had enough. I wanted to go home, not just on leave, but to stay home. At work and when off duty, my United Nations Military Observer (UNMO) teammates and I often sat in silence wondering if we would be spending Christmas in Sarajevo. I imagined that in these thoughtful moments, we were all questioning our reasons for being there. Our thoughts were the only place we could find solitude and feel our weaknesses and fears but, like good soldiers, we never showed our true feelings outwardly. The battle all boiled down to fight (should I stay and do my job?), flight (should I ask to go home?), or freeze (stay in Sarajevo and do nothing). For me and some of my mates, to run or show fear were not options.

For soldiers, the group, the pack, the solidarity, or the social pressure to do the right thing in the eyes of your peers holds your feet in place in times of peril. A soldier will overcome the urge to run in order to stay and fight because he doesn't want to let his buddies down. More than love of country, service to the army or to his regiment, the greatest factor enabling soldiers to hold their ground (or attack against perilous odds) is their mates. It's about doing the right thing, or even more practical: "I can die running away or stay here and die." Either way it sucks, but staying at your post is more honourable.

My symptoms came on slowly but they intensified with time. The mechanisms that protected my values and emotions all crashed at once. I had seen and experienced too much and no one could understand what had happened to me, least of all myself. I would battle the demons alone and would have to eventually admit to defeat. Courage or moral fibre is a finite human quality: if it could be held in a bucket and used wisely it would probably last a lifetime. But in the army, courage is not doled out in spoonfuls. In places like Sarajevo I used it by the cupful or by the litre. Then there were times when the bucket tipped over and it was empty. Try as I might, most times I ended up running on empty and was never given the chance for a refill. In the end, my biggest challenge would be to admit to myself that my bucket was empty.

I always had trouble describing my first impressions of Sarajevo. My mind was trying to find a place for my experiences in Bosnia. I put a lot of effort into downplaying my feelings by telling myself Bosnia was no big deal. But contradictions kept resurfacing, "No, Fred, this was something, but what?" I often felt overpowered by what I experienced. I can explain fear, happiness, anger, and so on, but what I could not explain was the mélange of emotions and feelings bouncing around in my head at once. Close to the surface were images and emotions that drove me to tears. Today they seem trivial: sights, sounds, and smells which in seconds could trigger a lump in my throat along with tears and an overpowering wave of sadness. What was happening to me?

Like most soldiers with an OSI, I thought I must be going crazy. My mind, heart, and soul hurt. On occasion I remember looking up to the sky and imploring God, "End it now! Stop fucking with my head!"

During my time in Sarajevo, my mind had clicked into survival mode, a mode that I had never experienced or maybe had not noticed before. For the next five years I would move through life as if on autopilot. I stumbled along on my backup primitive brain, which has the sole purpose of protecting me from physical and mental harm. The primitive brain was great when man ran with the wolves hundreds of years ago, or for me when I was moving about Bosnia during the war, which brought with it the constant threat of being killed.

The simple reactions of fight, flight, or freeze are what I returned to Canada with in summer of 1996. Caring, loving, feeling, and happiness had gone. Life had turned to black and white. I was physically back in Canada but my mind was still in the streets of Sarajevo. Family and friends avoided me, as I did them. They saw the change in me, but I did not want to admit to it and they were too afraid to ask what was wrong. My life was monotone, like my voice when I spoke of my time in Bosnia.

Only in my dreams, as I thrashed about in the dark, would my emotions kick in. It was a daily battle to keep myself together, almost to a point of physical and mental exhaustion, with the continued thought that I must be going crazy. I would rant and rave at the world and the people around me. I apologized a lot during those years, to the point where my apologies lost their meaning and sincerity. The people closest to me bore the brunt of my anger and no apologies could undo the harm I had done to them. There were many times I would ask God to just end it all, end my life and take the pain and confusion away. I thought I'd be better off dead.

My twenty-five years of soldiering had set me up for this crash. Army sayings like "Eat your weak," "Take the pain," "Suck it up, don't be weak" had come back to haunt me. I, like most soldiers, had built up an image of myself as tough and hard. And to an extent we are, but we are also human and only trained to be tough. I was confused and had no one to turn to. I wanted to run away but I was too good a soldier to run. When I left Bosnia sometime around the end of June 1996, almost one year to the day of my arrival, I felt nothing. I was numb. Going home was an anticlimax. I could have stayed another year in Bosnia and I still would have felt nothing.

The dreams began about eight months into my year in Bosnia. The bullet hits me in the back with such a force that I'm propelled forward as my legs collapse under me. The impact knocks the wind out of me and a searing pain instantly erupts from where the bullet strikes me. I fall forward, landing heavily on my right side, my helmeted head ricocheting off the pavement. I end up lying face down, my mind racing: the unimaginable has happened. "Fuck, I'm hit, fuck, fuck, fuck, get up, run, run!" my mind screams.

I struggle to get up. I force myself up but my hips and legs stay on the pavement. I can't move my legs, I can't feel them. Snap, another bullet passes by my head and strikes the pavement nearby. "No, please don't shoot. You fucking bastard, I can't move. Please let me get up and run. Where are my legs?" They are gone, my brain can't feel them anymore. Reality sets in. I'm going to die.

The second bullet hits me high up on my back around the left shoulder blade. In my semi pushup position I am corkscrewed around onto my back. The combination of the impact, the exiting of the bullet, and my turning motion causes a spray of blood to arc through the air. My fucking blood! My body and mind give up, I am dying. There is no pain, no sound, I just lie there. It's not supposed to end like this. My last sight will be of a grey sky over the city of Sarajevo. I feel cold. I'm so thirsty. What time is it at home? Janice has no idea that her husband of twenty-three years is dying. I'll never see her or Ben and Erin again. I feel so alone. My breathing is getting shallower, it's getting dark. "Christ, I'm cold."

I'm screaming. It's dark. Where am I?

"Fred, are you OK? Fuck, what's wrong?"

I'm gasping for air, I'm alive. "I'm OK," I snap back. "I'm OK, just a bad dream, sorry, go back to sleep, just a bad dream."

Sitting in the dark on the edge of my bunk I can hear my tentmates tossing and turning. They're all awake. Maybe they're embarrassed for me, or are they curious and maybe afraid of what I see when I dream? It's so fucking dark in here. I need air. I pull my pants on, slip my bare feet into my boots, and fumble my way outside for some air. The air is fresh and cool. I gulp it in and the night sky is clear and peppered with stars. My hands are shaking, my gut is knotted, my chest tight with anxiety and fear, but I am alive. I slump down on a bench exhausted and drained the same way I was at the end of every day in Sarajevo.

I was glad that first nightmare had come and gone in that dark tent at the Canadian camp in Klujuc, Bosnia. Little did I realize that it was the first of hundreds. In my dreams I would relive being shot at. Sometimes I would die, other times it would be a close call or someone else would die. I would be taken hostage and beaten, or maybe I'd find myself walking on a pile of corpses engulfed in the putrid stench of death. When the dreams focused on the dead, the stench was so real and powerful that I would wake up and puke. It was a never-ending cycle of dreams, demons, and tormentors each night. The dreams were vivid, terrifying, overloaded with all the sights, sounds, and smells of war. It always seemed so real, yet oddly enough I never feared sleep nor did I have any difficulty going to sleep. My problem was staying asleep. In that tent in Bosnia I did not know that I would never get a full night's sleep again.

You would think that after a year in Bosnia I'd have been excited about going home, yet I can't remember much about my departure or my trip home. I know Janice met me at the airport in Edmonton. Ben was working and Erin was off camping. No big deal, Dad had been away. It was as if I were a salesman back from a business trip. It was not their fault; they had no idea where I had been or what I had done. Throughout my time in the army I had deliberately kept my life as a soldier away from the "home front." When I think back, all I had secretly wanted from anyone was to be asked, "How was it and how are you doing?"

Upon my return from Bosnia in July 1996 I had no idea that I had already begun my trip down the road of the shell-shocked soldier. I was scared, ashamed, angry, tired, lonely, just engulfed in self-pity. Why me? Why did or how did I end up in that God-forsaken place? It simply boiled down to "Be careful what you ask for; you just may get it." I had asked for this posting as a UNMO and luck/ fate being what it is, I got it. In July 1995 I ended up in Sarajevo, Bosnia-Herzegovina.

The male ego also worked against me. For most men, especially those in the military, it is a sign of weakness to talk about your fears and emotions. Often you would lose it, there would be an extreme outburst of anger, a tirade for no apparent reason because the pressure to run and leave was ever present. We all wanted out, but with honour. My angry outbursts were scaring me. The anger seemed to boil up from the depths of my fears. I had no idea that such an intense feeling would not go away by just going home, and in reality my anger was only just beginning to cause me grief.

When I first returned home in July 1996 after my year in Bosnia, everything I had experienced was locked up inside me tight as a drum. When asked about my time in Bosnia I would talk about things that were humorous and I would tiptoe around anything serious. Naively, I thought I was opening up when I began offer up some of my feelings with unconnected bits of this and that. For the most part I let my thoughts and feelings run their course, mind-lessly letting things fall out. I came to realize that a lot of what I said was not being understood and I didn't expect it to be. Even today, fifteen years later, people feel uncomfortable when I talk about my experiences, even fellow soldiers.

Through trial and error I quickly learned to say very little. People couldn't relate and I didn't feel like putting the effort into explaining or describing what the war was like. There is a lot of baggage that I have yet to come to grips with, and a lot of what I've experienced is unexplainable. For the most part I'd downplay the whole thing, for their benefit or mine, I'm not really sure. Sometimes I sense that people may be hesitant or afraid to ask. Looking back, Janice, my wife, and my kids, Ben and Erin, seemed to realize that they should not bring up my time in Bosnia. Later, Janice would tell me that she immediately noticed changes in me, especially restlessness and aggression.

The added pressure and tension of returning home and leaving Bosnia actually began about a month before my departure. Upon my return, I was due to be posted (transferred) out of Edmonton back to an operational unit near Fredericton, New Brunswick, at Canadian Forces Base Gagetown. I was actually surprised and happy to be going back to my old unit, the 2nd Battalion of the Royal Canadian Regiment. What upset me was that I had to report by August 7. That would leave Janice and I only a month to take a house-hunting trip to Gagetown, purchase a house, come back, get the movers in, pack up, say goodbye to Ben and Erin who were staying in Edmonton, then drive from Edmonton to Fredericton, take possession of our house, and move in. All this after being away from my home and family for a year under some of the most stressful conditions a soldier could experience. What the fuck was the big hurry? All of the summer taskings would be over, I was going into the battalion transport officer's job which was no big deal, so why the rush?

Regardless of the appeals by my bosses in Bosnia, my request for a change of report date fell on deaf ears in Canada. The commanding officer (CO) was adamant that I report in on August 7. This type of attitude was coming from a CO I would quickly come to dislike and disrespect. Welcome home! Thank God Janice had a cooler approach to this military stupidity and would not sacrifice her time with me. We could have made the August 7 timing, but Janice said no. She said, "You go unaccompanied." This meant that after twelve months apart, she would say farewell to me again on August 6. I left for Gagetown and she remained in Edmonton. She would follow at the beginning of October. By doing this, she and I would have the better part of July to be together. When I thought about the situation, it had the smell of petty power-tripping and jealousy on the part of the Commanding Officer, and this only became more evident once I arrived in Gagetown.

In my mental state upon returning to Canada, going back to an infantry battalion was the best thing for me. The rhythm of the day-to-day goings on were familiar and comforting. And I need a routine to get through the everyday crap of peacetime soldiering. There was no challenge in going back to a unit, but this was good for me at that point.

My concentration and my concern for day-to-day life were buried somewhere deep inside me. The other plus at Gagetown was the familiar faces of the soldiers and officers I had served with in the past. However, I would find that I had very little in common with them. Today when I reflect on that time, I realize I may have been perceived as arrogant. In my mind they could never understand what I had seen and experienced. I drew away from my old friendships and fostered very few new ones. Oh, I was civil and as friendly as I could be, but there was a void between us. In an almost child-like way I looked on the officers I worked with with contempt. No one asked me to tell my story, therefore in my mind no one cared. It was as if I wanted them to read my mind. This need to tell my story gnawed at me constantly and brought on an anger and resentment that I often brought home with me and wrongly dumped on Janice.

At work, I preferred the company of the soldiers to that of my fellow officers. Work was my way of coping with the demons. I could move through the day avoiding situations that I would come to know as "triggers." I relaxed in the soldiers' company because being commissioned as an officer from the ranks gave me an insider's knowledge of their language and the way they thought. I enjoyed their no-nonsense approach to the profession of soldiering and deep down I knew that the soldiers had a better appreciation and understanding of those missions than the officers. All I felt from the officers was jealousy and envy of what I had experienced, whereas the soldiers, because of my background and experience, trusted me. Christ, what I had experienced was ripping the guts out of me and if left to follow its own course, would destroy me and my family.

CHAPTER 14
PISSED OFF

Jerry Deveau had served in Rwanda during the genocide and remained there for six months. At the time of this incident he was a captain with thirty-five years of service. For the past three years Jerry had been actively involved in his therapy. His psychologist, Doctor Joyce Belliveau, told him that he was making steady progress and she felt that he had turned the corner with his OSI.

So it was a complete surprise when, on a Friday afternoon, Brenda, his wife, took a call for him at home and was told that Jerry was no longer to attend therapy with Dr. Belliveau. Brenda was upset. She knew that a change of therapists would really affect the progress that Jerry had made over the past year. When Jerry got home she told him about the call. Jerry lost it and called the mental health clinic. It being Friday afternoon all he got was a voice message telling him that the clinic was closed and to call back on Monday. From personal experience I know that calling on a Friday afternoon is a tactic used by managers when delivering bad news. It allows the recipient to blow their stack, rant and rave, and hopefully run out of steam over the weekend and calm down before they confront the system on Monday.

Even though they had Jerry's work phone number they had deliberately called his home phone. Jerry knew that they had done this to avoid being confronted and to avoid being caught up in the shit storm they knew this cancellation would cause.

Big mistake pulling that tactic with Jerry.

His weekend was not spent letting off steam; on the contrary it just fuelled the fire and Jerry was ready to explode as he drove to the mental health clinic on Monday. There was no one there so Jerry headed to the base medical clinic to talk with the commanding officer. Luckily for the CO, he was away, as was the base psychiatrist. Instead, Jerry cornered Dr. Vardy, who he knew. He told him how his wife had taken a call on Friday from a therapist at the mental health clinic and was told that a case management meeting had been held to discuss his treatment and that they had decided to stop his therapy and transfer him to the base clinic. Supposedly, in attendance at the case meeting was a psychologist Jerry had never met and the base mental health administrator, who is not a clinician. Those not in attendance were the base psychiatrist, Jerry's doctor, and his therapist, Dr. Belliveau. In fact, when Jerry spoke with Joyce she said she had no idea that his treatment was to cease. Dr. Vardy told him that there was little he could do, but he put him in contact with a Ms. Simms who handled complaints related to base health services.

Jerry told her in soldier speak (a plethora of four-letter, off-colour words usually delivered in a loud voice) that he was getting fucked around and that if he did not see the CO by 1300 he was heading into the CBC station to let them know what was going on. With that promise he left and went to work

He was angry that after all his work and progress his anger and anxiety management was gone. He was ready to "fuck somebody up" when his phone rang. On the other end was the base medical clinic sergeant major (MWO, the highest non-commissioned officer) at the clinic. The MWO asked if he could come over and discuss the situation with Jerry, but Jerry repeated his "1300 I'll be at the CBC." The MWO came to see Jerry at work. Jerry respected the MWO because he was not one of the "pencil-necked assholes," so he took

the time to bring him up to speed on what was going on. He finished by telling him that there was no fucking way he was going to
accept a decision made by an unknown psychologist and a paper-
pusher without consulting his psychiatrist, doctor, and therapist.
The MWO took it all in and said he would be picking the CO up at
the airport later on and promised to pass on what was going on.
Jerry made sure he repeated his plan that if by 1300 there was no
answer, they would see him on the six o'clock news.

The MWO met the CO, who immediately called Jerry and brokered
a deal that he would gather all of the info and they would meet
tomorrow at 0800. Jerry cut him some slack and agreed to skip his
visit to the CBC studio and meet with the CO the following morning.

Jerry arrived on the stroke of eight and was ushered into the
CO's office. Jerry had thirty-five years of service and experience and
easily sensed that the CO was taking the condescending approach,
to the effect that "I can sort this out and I will make you go away,
Captain Deveau."

The meeting begins with the CO offering Jerry a seat and as soon
as Jerry's butt is in it, the CO stands up and begins to talk as he
walks around his office. Jerry stands up and the CO asks him to
"please sit down, Captain Deveau."

"No, sir."

The CO is shocked. Then Jerry launches into soldier speak. "If
you think for one fucking moment that you are going to intimidate
me by walking around your office as I sit there and you talk down
to me, you are fucking wrong and the meeting is over."

"Captain Deveau, there must be a misunderstanding."

"No there fucking isn't. You are wasting my time. You don't
seem to have an answer, so at 1300 I'll be in town talking with a
friend of mine who is the CBC morning show host and I will tell the
public how fucked up the mental health clinic is."

Next, the inexperienced CO uses what he feels is his trump card.
"Captain Deveau, you know I can talk to your CO about this rude
behaviour," he says.

"Go the fuck ahead. Here's his phone number and I can tell you that this kind of bullshit may work with some soldiers, but not with this one. Go ahead and charge me with insubordination if you want. However, it will probably be your first time standing in front of the base commander and wasting his time sorting out the shit storm you call a mental health clinic. Now why don't you sit down and I'll tell you what I want."

The CO realizes that the battle is lost and the situation now dictates that he sit down. "I want to know who was at my case management meeting and why my psychologist, psychiatrist, and doctor were not invited. I also want to know why the paperwork terminating my therapy was signed by the administrator who has no qualifications to even be in the meeting let alone sign off on ending my therapy with Dr. Belliveau."

Then Jerry gets up and storms out of the office. But he is still a man on a mission and he heads to the mental health clinic to confront the administrator. He corners him in his office and asks him why he signed off on the cease treatment paperwork. The administrator vehemently denies doing so. He said he wasn't even at the meeting. Jerry knows this is a lie. Earlier, Jerry had called a friendly employee at the clinic and they confirmed that the administrator had been there. Jerry tells him that he is full of shit and before leaving makes a point of telling him, "I am going to continue to see Joyce until she says that my treatment is over." Jerry eventually talks with the base psychiatrist who says he is never invited to case management meetings, which Jerry says is bullshit. Bewildered, Jerry repeated what he had said to the administrator and reiterated that he would be seeing Dr. Belliveau that week.

Later in the week, Jerry attended his scheduled session with Joyce and they talked about the ethics and the damage caused when a person, through no choice of their own, is made to change therapists. Prior to this incident Jerry was doing well and probably would have been switched to monthly therapy sessions. However, the arbitrary decision to fuck him around opened up some old wounds.

Like many soldiers, it had taken Jerry several years of misery before he stepped forward for help. He had been working hard to come to grips with his trauma and the stress caused by trying to keep his illness hidden and under control for so long. The clinical term "secondary wounding" refers to the damage to a soldier as a result of such things as stopping therapy or people doubting your illness. Many health care professionals and military members feel that anyone with PTSD is faking the symptoms for a diagnosis which they then can use to apply to Veterans Affairs for a pension. Basically, they think the sufferer is in it for the money. The secondary wounding as a result of stigma can be compared to a boxer in the tenth round who is on his way to winning when BANG: a punch gets through and he staggers back on his heels and what he thought was a sure thing suddenly isn't.

Jerry had been blindsided, but he pulled through it because he was a no-nonsense combat engineer with thirty-five years' service who had nothing to lose. At the opposite end of OSI treatment is the private or corporal with four or five years' service faced with a situation like Jerry's. I know what happens because I've seen it played during my time as a peer support coordinator. These soldiers typically walk away, saying, "Fuck it, they had their chance."

It was quite obvious to me what was going on. It was about the money, not about care or support for the injured. It was some bean-counter trying to impress his boss by showing him how much money his decisive decisions had saved the Crown.

I was unaware of the hassles that were taking place on the base. However, during this period I talked with several soldiers who were concerned about seeing a part-time psychiatrist instead of starting regular therapy with a therapist. They said all the psychiatrist did was tinker with their medication. Some told me they were in therapy and when I asked who with, they said the mental health nurses that had been recently hired at the base. I advised them to demand that they be assigned a therapist because mental health nurses are not qualified therapists. I did discuss the part-time psychiatrist situation with the mental health clinic administrator and asked who would be replacing the psychiatrist (who was leaving because his license to practice had been revoked in Newfoundland for having an affair with one of his patients). However, my main concern was whether they were ready for the return of the 2 RCR battle group from Afghanistan which would begin in August 2007. The administrator assured me that they had a plan, but did not or could not offer me any of the details. The clinic was struggling to hire more staff, in some cases people with little or no experience in trauma therapy. They had hired mental health nurses who are not qualified to conduct therapy, social workers, recent graduates from university, and psychologists with no experience in trauma therapy. This was the situation at most military bases. Money had been allocated to hire more mental health therapists so that there would be approximately 450 therapists in the Forces. Even this past year the military was called onto the mat by an all-party government committee to answer to the fact that they were still almost 100 therapists shy of the 450 they had the funds to hire. The standard answer given is: "We are still trying to source more mental health workers, because we are committed to the health and welfare of our men and women of the Forces."

CHAPTER 15

JACQUES, ROYAL CANADIAN MOUNTED POLICE CONSTABLE

A llow me to set the stage. When the OSISS Program was first launched, it was decided that because the Royal Canadian Mounted Police (RCMP) were considered veterans upon retirement or release and entitled to veterans benefits, then they would also be entitled to our services. The RCMP leadership was not keen on having military veterans helping their members, especially those who were still serving. We thought the military treated its soldiers badly when it came to PTSD, but we were shocked by the "eat your weak" treatment of RCMP members with PTSD. Within the leadership of the Force there was no empathy or sympathy for members afflicted with a mental health injury. They were ignored, spurned, seen as weak, and considered an embarrassment. Like the mentally injured military members, constables were very reluctant to step forward and seek help because they knew that they would be treated as if they were faking their injury and in all likelihood would be released from the police force.

The fear of being found out is how I came to meet Jacques, an RCMP member with over twenty years of loyal service.

It was in the first week of January 2007 when I received a call from Marc, the peer support coordinator in Quebec City. After exchanging our New Year's niceties he told me about Jacques. Marc had received a call from a friend he had served with who said that his brother, Jacques, had crashed and burned (a term we use for someone who has completely collapsed mentally) and he needed help but was afraid to approach his employers, the RCMP.

Jacques was on Christmas leave at his brother's place in Montreal and his brother did not know how to help him. Marc advised him that the best thing was to get Jacques back home to Moncton, New Brunswick, and have him admitted to a hospital. Once Jacques was back in NB I'd provide peer support while Marc got the wheels rolling to have Jacques admitted to a treatment program at Veterans Affairs Canada's Paul Triquet VC Centre in Quebec City. The treatment program would stabilize Jacques, sort out medication, deal with any dependencies, and then begin therapy. The centre is the number one treatment facility for French-speaking Veterans in Canada, which in my eyes meant Jacques would most likely make it through his crisis.

Two days later, I received a call from Marc who said Jacques was back in New Brunswick and had been admitted to the Georges Dumont Hospital psych ward in Moncton. That is where I visited him the next day. The drive from my place to Moncton is a little over an hour and very boring, which allowed me to contemplate what state I would find Jacques in. Being able to see him meant that he was out of isolation, but more than likely he would be heavily medicated. I hoped that he would be able to provide me with the required info to fill out the paperwork for Veterans Affairs.

When I arrived at the George Dumont Hospital, I made my way to the psych ward and spoke with a nurse. I explained who I was and what I did. She asked no questions, but led me to a small room where she said I could talk to Jacques in private. My first sight of Jacques was as he made his way down the hallway accompanied by an orderly. He was dressed in blue hospital pajamas and slippers. His gait was slow and he shuffled like a convict in chains. The orderly had a tight grip on his elbow and Jacques' head was wobbling as if he were drunk. The orderly sat him down and said, "Call me when you're done." Then he turned and left the room.

I said nothing for a few moments, just letting Jacques absorb his new surroundings. He slowly lifted his head and I said, "Hello, Jacques." There was no immediate response as Jacques squinted, trying to focus on who had spoken. Jacques was a big man, well over six feet, a bit overweight, unshaven, with hair longer than one would expect on an RCMP member. His shoulders drooped and he looked totally defeated, like a boxer sitting in his corner knowing he'd lost his fight but still had another round to go.

I said hi again and this time Jacques lifted his head and looked at me. "Hi, Jacques, my name is Fred Doucette. I'm with OSISS and I am here to help you." I reached out, offering a handshake. Jacques looked at my hand for a moment, then slowly raised his hand. His handshake was weak, which was to be expected of a person who is heavily medicated, but I knew that it felt reassuring to him. I did not launch into the usual spiel about who I was and what OSISS was, that would come another day. Right now all I said was "How are you doing?" Jacques said nothing for a moment, then almost whispering said, "I'm pretty fucked up." From those four words I knew that in his mind he had nothing to live for, was no longer the person he used to be, and thought that everyone in his life would be better off if he were dead. I was not surprised when he began to cry. Through the tears he said, "I've got nothing to live for."

I let Jacques cry for a few moments before I said, "Jacques, I was where you are eight years ago and that is why I'm able to be here to help and listen to you, because I know that you can get your life back. Right now you're as low as you can be and feel that there's no help, that no one cares, and there's no future." Jacques sat up as if struck by lightning. He lifted his head, looked me in the eyes, and in a clear voice said, "That's it, that's it." We had connected and I knew from experience that his healing had begun simply because he knew he was no longer alone.

Most peers, once they've connected with you, want to tell you their story and what led them to where they were now. Normally I tell them that they don't have to tell me their story. All I have to do is ask them where they served and I know most of what led to their injury. Jacques' story was different. He would be the first non-military peer that I had worked with so I let him tell me. He had twenty-two years of service with the RCMP and had done a myriad of jobs over those years. At present he was with the Moncton highway detachment. Jacques' words were a bit slurred and he knew they were, so he paused often to organize his thoughts.

Jacques fell silent, and then he scared the shit out of me when he almost yelled my name. "Fred!" Then, without hesitating, he began. "I was on three weeks' Christmas leave, relaxing and glad to be away from highway policing over the holidays which can be a real mess, you know what I mean?" I nodded. Jacques let out a burst of air like a weightlifter who has just dropped a four hundred-pound barbell onto the floor. His eyes were scanning and blinking. "It's OK, Jacques, relax, take your time, we're in no hurry." He drew in a couple of deep breaths, shifted in his chair, and looked straight at me with a look of relief on his face. Looking me in the eye meant that he had begun to trust me and most likely he sensed I would not judge him as he told me his story.

"So I was on holidays, my wife was at work, and my kids were still in school, so I had the house to myself and all was good. One morning after everyone had left, I made another coffee and sat down to watch some TV. I scrolled the channels, most had the news on, crappy morning shows, and kids cartoons, until I landed on one of those true crime shows. I should have turned the TV off, but what the hell, I had nothing else to do." He sat across from me, his eyes straight ahead, looking through me back to the past, gathering his words, putting them in order, then summoning up the courage to tell me about the trauma that now consumed him. Taking a deep breath and letting it out slowly, he began. "I was a brand new constable. I had only been on the job for a week or two. I was patrolling when the dispatcher sent me to a house where a woman had had a heart attack and the ambulance was on its way. I hit the lights and headed to the house, only a few kilometres away. I was there in a couple of minutes and pulled into the driveway of an older farmhouse and told dispatch that I was on the scene. I got out of my cruiser and walked to the house. I remember thinking, OK, CPR, remember how it's done, keep her alive until the ambulance arrives, be the hero, blah, blah, blah, and no big deal. I was a typical new cop, young and cocky." Now he stared at me as the sights, sounds, smells, the memory of that day became focused. Knowing this was a critical moment I asked him if he was OK. We can take a break, take it easy, remember we're in no hurry. Jacques gave a sigh and said, "No, Fred, I have to tell you. It's here," pointing to his head, "I've got to let it out." OK, just relax and take your time.

He began in a clear voice. "I go up the back stairs onto the deck. I should have paid more attention to the dozen or so empty cases of beer and the other crap on the property and under the back deck. Maybe it would have put me on guard, but it didn't because they don't teach you that at the RCMP Depot. Those clues you have to learn on the job." Jacques closed his eyes, did a few neck rotations, and took in a few deep breaths, exhaled and began. "I knocked on the door and said, 'It's the police.' There was no immediate response, so I banged on the door again and it opened.

"A middle-aged man stood in the doorway, tall and fit but unshaved and dressed in a T-shirt and sweatpants. Where's your wife, I asked as he closed the door behind me, then without a word, BANG! He hits me in the back of the head and sends me flying into the kitchen table. Weird, but I remember my stupid hat flying off as I shook off the shock of the hit. I quickly turned around, more in shock and in response to being hit from behind and in doing so I came face to face with the fellow, who is standing in front of the door with a knife in his hand. I don't remember any details but I know that I didn't even think of drawing my gun, then he was coming at me again. Thank God for the table because I managed to get on the other side of it and out of range of the stabbing and slashing he was making at me. Staying alive was all I could think of and where was the fucking ambulance?

At some point, as we danced around the table, he slipped and I managed to flip the table over on top of him and sandwiched him between it and the floor. I saw the knife in his hand so I put all my weight on that side and forced the edge of the table onto his forearm. He let go of the knife and tried to pull his arm under the table. No fucking way, I thought. Just then I heard the ambulance siren as well as the distinctive sound of a police cruiser siren. One of the ambulance attendants was banging on the door as I was yelling to come in, and when he did he stopped in his tracks when he saw me on the floor with a table on top of my pissed-off attacker. Seconds later the constable arrived, pushed his way through, and without hesitating he kicked the knife away, kneeled on the attacker's arm, pinning it to the floor, and snapped a handcuff on his wrist. We yelled for him to keep still or else we'd beat the fucking shit out of him. He went limp as a wet noodle and he didn't move a muscle or resist in any way, the fight was out of him.

I got onto the radio and called for more backup when the paramedics found a woman lying on the floor with multiple stab wounds. His wife was dead and the house now became a murder scene. We took the fellow out, put him in the cruiser, and only then did I exhale and realize what had just happened. That's when my hands began to shake. The duty sergeant came over and asked if I was OK. I said, I'm OK. And I went back to the detachment to fill out a report. I was back at work the next day as if nothing had happened and wrote it off as just part of the job."

Jacques closed his eyes and he took a deep breath, I knew he was reliving the exact moment and the feeling you get when you know that you are *not* going to die. Sometimes it is the only positive memory that you can pull from the depths of your depression and misery. You cannot handle the moment before or after your near-death incident. All you can feel is, it wasn't your day to die. Jacques' eyes were closed, he was silent. I knew he was recovering or better still, was pulling his shit together. I said nothing, just sat there quietly, waiting for him to carry on.

When Jacques opened his eyes he looked shocked and confused, not really sure of what had just happened. After a few moments he said, "I'm sorry that I dumped what happened to me, you must have heard a lot worse."

"Well, Jacques, we try not to rate the trauma, to us it's trauma just like cancer is cancer, there are no points given for severity. Now it is totally up to you if you want to carry on and tell me what happened last week when you were watching TV." He shifted in his chair and looked out of the window at the grey cold January day and said, "Well, on the forensic program they were talking about the various kinds of evidence that can be gathered at a crime scene. Nothing shocking, just a bunch of guys in lab coats looking into microscopes, pretty boring stuff, I thought. I was about to change the station when the narrator said that the science of blood splatter evidence has become one of the most useful pieces of evidence that can be recovered from a crime scene. All I had to do, Fred, was to press the remote and I wouldn't be sitting here today."

"What do you mean, Jacques?"

"Fred, the narrator went on to say that the first time blood splatter evidence was used in court was twenty years ago on a case involving the murder of a woman. There on the TV was the crime scene video of that incident I was involved with twenty-two years ago. In an instant everything crashed back like waves on a rocky shore. I was flashing back to fatal car accidents, drownings, murders, fires, child abuse, rape, everything. Fred, all of those buried memories were there, they had never really gone away.

"Alone at home, all of the guilt, fear, anger, just kept rolling in. One minute I was crying like a baby, the next I was raving like a mad man. What the fuck is happening to me? was the only rational thought that I could muster. I went upstairs, got a beer, and paced the floor, drinking beer after beer, talking to myself. Am I going mad? What's happening to me? Then I began to cry as the images of kids ripped apart in traffic accidents, drowned bloated bodies, bodies burnt beyond recognition, bruised and beaten women and children, young women beaten and raped. Fred, it was all there.

"When my wife came home I was drunk and pretty fucked up. I managed to convince her that a couple of friends dropped by and we had a few beers and my edginess was due to a crappy sleep last night. I knew that she didn't believe me but thankfully she didn't pursue it. I held it together for Christmas and we headed to my brother's for New Year's where I got really pissed and totally broke down. Now I'm in the hospital all fucked up on medication and terrified about the future, if there is a future."

Jacques closed his eyes, let out a big sigh, and began to cry. Whatever energy he'd had was all used up by telling his story. Again I said nothing. Jacques would decide if he wanted to talk or go back to his room. I was surprised that he had managed to tell me what he did. Most of the fellows I dealt with were tired of telling their story or they could not put their trauma into words. It didn't matter to me, I was just glad that they had reached out for help.

"Fred, look at me crying like a baby in a mental ward. What the fuck happened?"

"Jacques, you are a strong, brave man who has seen and experienced so much that your brain can't take anymore. There isn't a person on this earth that does not have a breaking point, regardless of how strong they think they are. Christ, Jacques, you kept over twenty-two years of trauma locked away in your memories and now there is no room left. In fact, your cup has run over."

Jacques sat staring at me, eyes wide open, nodding his head in agreement. "Fred, that's what happened. It was like the dam burst and I couldn't control what came down the river."

I knew that Jacques was exhausted and I didn't want to pressure him, so I pulled out the papers for his VAC application and got him to give me the tombstone data (name, date of birth, etc.). "So, Jacques," I said, "here is the plan. It's simple and your part in it is to take your medication and work at getting your mental health back. You will get your life back, but it will be a rough road. The therapy will open up old wounds and there will be times when you will feel like you're not moving forward but sliding back and that is normal. When that happens, keep fighting, stay positive, and remember you will get better. Don't worry about getting admitted to the Triquet Centre, Marc is handling that. I will put the paperwork in to VAC, and I will visit your wife with an OSISS family support coordinator. Your job is to focus on your therapy."

I called the orderly and as we waited I told Jacques that he was not alone and that from here on his life would start to come back together. Jacques shook my hand as the tears welled up in his eyes. I knew the tears were not from desperation but from hope.

I did not see Jacques for over a year. I visited his wife with a family peer support coordinator several days after I met him and by that time he was in the Triquet Centre in Quebec City. His wife said that he had sounded a lot better when he called the day before and that she knew that he would work hard at whatever they asked him to do.

A year or so had passed and one day I was having lunch with my wife at a restaurant in Fredericton. When I went to the cash to pay my bill, a fellow behind me said, "Fred, how are you?" When I turned I did not know who he was. "Fred, it's me, Jacques." I know that he savoured the moment, especially when I didn't recognize him. There he stood, crisp white shirt, haircut, shaved, with a big shit-eating grin on his face. He grabbed my hand and there was strength in his grip and he wouldn't let go. He kept shaking it and asked me how I was doing.

"Christ, never mind me, look at you. You're doing really well. What's going on with you? " I paid my bill and we stepped outside and he told me that everything had worked out and he felt great, almost giddy at being able to say he was OK.

"I just finished my return to full duties medical, and all is well, so I can get back to work with a whole new outlook on life and I feel stronger. It was a tough year, but I could feel myself getting better each day. I also know that there is no cure for PTSD. You get better, but if I'm not careful it can sneak up on me. My family life is great, they now have this new rejuvenated father and husband who loves them dearly and who savours every day he is with them. As for work, well, let's say that if it were not for some friends in high places I'd probably be a civilian today. But that crap is behind me. In fact, I remember you telling me that you can't change the past but what you do today can influence the future. Fred, if it weren't for you, Marc, and my brother, I would be dead today. That visit you made to me in the hospital even though I was all fucked up gave me a glimmer of hope and, my friend, I guess that is what I needed." Jacques put out his hand to shake mine then pulled me in and gave me a big hug and said, "Thank you."

CHAPTER 16
SEXUAL ASSAULT

During the war in Bosnia the Serbian military used rape as a weapon of war. Women were raped as Serb soldiers moved through an area, or they were taken to the various rape centres that were established throughout the country. In 1996 just after the war ended, I was part of the NATO Implementation Force and on several occasions I was tasked to investigate various sites that were alleged to be rape centres. One that still haunts me was in an elementary school.

There were blood-stained mattresses strewn throughout the classrooms, hundreds of empty liquor bottles littered the place, and the tattered remnants of women's clothing was strewn about. It was an evil place. Silently, my driver and I walked through the building, unable to imagine the horror, fear, and pain of the women and girls that were brought into this hell. After we left he broke the silence and asked why these rape centres existed at all.

On a previous tour of Bosnia I had learned that rape was used as a punishment, to impregnate Bosnian women so they would mother a Serbian child, and also for the sexual gratification of Serbian soldiers. The women who survived these rape factories were shunned by their communities because their children were half Serbian. Never mind that these children were the result of rape and not from collusion with the enemy. In most cases the women were seen as damaged goods, especially the young unmarried women. There have been estimates of how many were raped, but there are no estimates on how many abortions were carried out and how many women died of rape or as a result of a botched abortion.

The rape centres, as heinous as they were, were considered an act of war and a war crime. There were too few criminals brought to The Hague by the International Crimes Tribunal who were found guilty and punished for their war crimes which included rape. And the attention given to the war crime trials by the media was next to nothing. There were the odd splashes in the media when one of the big fish, like Mladic, were reeled in, but other than that there was very little coverage.

My experience with rape in war did not prepare me to deal with the sexual assault and rape of women in the Canadian military by their peers. I couldn't wrap my mind around what it must be like when your OSI is the result of sexual assault by a fellow member of the Canadian Forces. After dealing with several victims of sexual assault through my work with OSSIS, I came to realize that there is a whole strata of OSIs related to sexual assault by a peer while deployed on operations. What really angered me was the extent the military went in keeping the subject under the radar.

On the battlefield justice can be immediate and swift — the enemy will pay for your OSI. In some way you can tell yourself that your OSI was the price for doing your job as a soldier, or a leader of soldiers, when the shit hit the fan. Where and who do soldiers with PTSD from sexual assault get their justice from? Their terrorist comes home with them and whether their assailant is charged depends upon the courage of the victim. The stigma attached to an OSI is extremely difficult to cope with but when the OSI manifests as a result of sexual assault, the depth of the stigma is multiplied tenfold. Not only does the victim have to deal with the OSI, they also have to deal with fear of coming forward and pressing charges.

The perpetrators of sexual assault on operations are predators who have planned and taken advantage of the environment their victims find themselves in. The assaults are not random attacks, but are carefully planned, well calculated, and aimed at taking advantage of the fear and the loneliness of being deployed. In many cases, the perpetrator is in a position of power. They may hold a higher rank, which may be used to intimidate the victim before, during, and after the assault. The cases I worked on all involved someone of a lower rank being assaulted by someone of a higher rank.

JANE

I was first introduced to Jane one afternoon at the office. She was talking to my colleague and I knew that the conversation was serious because my colleague was very formal when he introduced me. When I shook Jane's hand I noticed that her eyes were red and that there was a box of tissues beside her chair. Reading the scene, I realized that the conversation must be quite serious and that they would be better off if I wasn't there. So I exited and went for a coffee.

The next time I met Jane was at the OSISS group gathering, which takes place every Tuesday evening. Although the group was mostly men, it wasn't unusual to have a woman there and it was good to see that she was put at ease within minutes. She once told the group this was the only place where she laughed.

There are usually eight to ten serving soldiers or veterans that drop by each Tuesday, and it's an open meeting, so you can come and go as you like. We're there strictly for peer support, specifically social support, and there are only two rules: first, no talking about trauma and second, no discussion about money from pensions and the like. Everybody adheres to the rules, so we talk about everything from sports to movies, and as a group we all get along quite well. The only qualification required to attend is that you have to have been diagnosed with an OSI and be in therapy.

We gabbed about this and that and over the course of the evening I found out that Jane was forty-ish, had been married twice, served ten years in the logistic branch of the army, and had done two tours of duty in Afghanistan. She, like the rest of us, had been released from the CAF as a result of having been diagnosed with PTSD. Over the weeks she shared a few more details: she was a grandmother, was in the process of getting a divorce from her second husband, and lived nearby in Oromocto West.

When I began writing this chapter I approached her and asked if she would be interested in telling her story, to add another first-hand account to my book—a woman's perspective on her OSI from her second tour of Afghanistan. She said she would get back to me, but she never did, which didn't surprise me. Some people are very guarded about what has happened to them or simply tired of telling their story.

At our first group meeting in January 2015, Jane was sitting next to me and, as usual, the group had fragmented into several one-on-one conversations. We talked about the holiday season and the ups and downs that come with it. At one point Jane asked me, "How's the book going?" I said it was moving on and I asked her once again if she would be interested in having her story told. Jane said she was ready share her story.

That evening she told me she had been raped by another soldier while on her second tour to Afghanistan. I was a shocked but not entirely surprised, because although it is one of the most despicable crimes that can occur in a unit, it does occur. We did not talk about the details. Jane told me that the day over a year ago when I had first met her was the day before she was to meet with military police. A National Investigative Service (NIS) team was being sent down from Ottawa to interview her. That interview was the first time she had talked about the rape.

I had already started a chapter on rape but I didn't have a first-hand account from a woman who had been raped. I said that I would email her what I had in the chapter to date so she could see where I was going with it and if she still was interested then we could meet. We met on January 21, and spent about two hours discussing her PTSD.

Jane had deployed to Afghanistan for her second tour in March 2010. She said that the first tour had been exciting because it was her first deployment. However, she said, "When I got off of the plane on my second tour I was hit by the heat, smells, dust, and dirt and I felt this tour was going to be different." In no time her work settled into a rhythm and everyone worked hard and kept busy because it made the time go by faster.

In June, she was raped by her superior where she worked. It happened at night and he planned it so that they were alone. He had spent months planning how, when, and where he would rape her. As we talked Jane said that she didn't want to discuss any of the details of the actual rape. I agreed. I knew reliving it was something she and her psychologist would work on.

In the days following the rape Jane said, "I didn't know what to do. Should I report it? Will it be a he said she said? There were no witnesses, and I still had to work with my rapist. I was confused and terrified, so I did what the majority of women do who are raped. I said nothing.

"The days and weeks went by. My rapist carried on as if nothing had happened, content in the knowledge that I had and probably would not report the rape. Living in terror, I felt sure that he would do it again and I began to fear for my life. The only place that I felt safe was in the toilet because it had a door that could be locked. In the evening I would disappear for hours hiding in the toilet with my rifle, which I doubted I'd ever use to defend myself." Jane had been issued and trained to use a rifle but never imagined that she'd have to use it to defend herself from a peer.

"Our sleeping accommodation was in tents and thankfully they were not coed. Regardless, there was no privacy, just a blanket between the beds. We used pallets on the floor to keep the mud and water at bay in our bed spaces. At night when everyone was fast asleep, I couldn't sleep because I would lay there terrified because I knew he would walk through our tent at some point during the night. I would hear the tent door open, then the creaking of the pallets, then silence as he stopped and stood at the foot of my bunk. I was so fucking scared that I slept with my rifle still wondering what I'd do with it if he attacked me again. I was always tired and on edge because it wasn't until my body forced me to shut down that I got any rest.

"About three weeks after I was raped, I had yet to say anything about what had happened to me. My rapist continued to stalk and torment me. He would brush up against me or stand behind me with his hand on my shoulder asking questions. He would even send me suggestive emails from his desk, which was about six feet from my desk. The stress and fear just kept going on and on.

"Nothing had changed. To leadership I was just a stressed-out woman and we'll keep an eye on her. In hindsight I have wondered what would have happened if I had said I was raped. Would I have been treated better? I had already started lining up reasons and excuses why I should keep my mouth shut and the overriding reason was, what about my career?

"The officer in charge of our unit noticed that I had changed and that I seemed really stressed out, and with the encouragement of my rapist, who worked for the captain, I was ordered to see a doctor who then handed me off to a social worker. I was not forced to tell them why I was stressed, but he had them take my rifle away from me for my own safety. Once they took my rifle away from me I felt helpless. In my mind I had nothing left to protect me from another attack. It was then that I had to end the hell and my only way out was suicide.

"I don't even remember when I tried to kill myself, all I remember is waking up in our camp hospital. I was really fucked up. When my head cleared there beside my bed holding my hand was my rapist. I was terrified. When I looked around thankfully there were other people in my room. He dropped my hand, smiled, and stepped away. My rapist was there to gloat and to make sure his power over me was complete. He smiled and left the room, knowing that he had won.

"It only took a few days for my unit to have me on a plane with an escort to an American base hospital for my safety. We arrived and it took a few minutes for us to realize that they had no idea of who we were and what we were doing there. By chance a Canadian liaison officer spotted us and sorted things for us. I spent a few days there and I thought that the hospital had no idea who we were because my unit just wanted to get me out of their responsibility. The American hospital made sure that the large American military hospital in Frankfurt, Germany, knew we were coming. I flew into Germany and I was kept there and eventually was shipped home with my escort.

"I thought that putting distance between me and my rapist would make things easier, but it didn't. I was still afraid of him finding me and raping me again. The armed forces is not big and there is no place to hide. When I arrived home I found out that I had been immediately placed on a permanent medical category."

This was completely out of line with the way a career is normally ended for medical reasons. Jane should have been placed on a temporary category for six months, then medically assessed and placed on a second temporary category for six months, then assessed for a third time. Only then would they assign you a permanent category. Jane was placed on a permanent category and the wheels were put in motion to have her released from the CF.

Within a month of being repatriated from Afghanistan, Jane was sent to a private civilian treatment centre in Ontario, called Homewood. The program she was put on at Homewood lasted a month. You lived in and your days were structured as if you were in school. The centre provides treatment for police, paramedics, nurses, firemen, and serving soldiers and veterans suffering with PTSD. There is another centre in Guelph, Ontario, called Bellwood and as of late there is a waiting list for both centres of up to a year.

For the most part, they do great work in rehabilitating those with
PTSD.

"When I returned to Comox I felt a bit better, but it was all I
could do to keep my head above water, because the fear which is
overpowering was always swirling around in my head. I was on
medical leave and on doctors' orders to stay off of the base and I
was excused from having to wear a uniform." Some severely traumatized soldiers cannot put on the uniform because it triggers
their trauma. However, if their therapy goes well, some of them
return to work in uniform.

Jane said that her husband was also in the military and was
given a week off when she arrived home from Homewood. "He was
ordered to stay at home so he could keep an eye on me 24 and 7. His
reaction said a lot. He was pissed off and angry because he could
not leave me alone at home. His anger confirmed what his true
colours were and I knew that when I went east he would not be
coming with me. I had suspicions that he had been cheating on me
while I was in Afghanistan, and I was proved right when I caught
him and his new woman having sex in our garage during the week
he was home with me. When he came in he said, 'It's not what it
seems.' No, it was exactly what it was, he was a cheating bastard.

"I knew my career was over, as was my marriage, and I did
not want to remain in Comox so I requested a posting to the Joint
Personnel Support Unit (JPSU) at Base Gagetown, New Brunswick.
They refused my request based on the cost to post me back east
where I wished to live after my release. However, they did allow
me to use my relocation move, which everyone gets when they are
released from the military. That really confirmed that I was being
punted once they got the paperwork sorted out.

"Before I moved east, an incident occurred at Forces Base
Comox that really shook me. The MWO, who was technically my
boss, called me and ordered me to come onto the base dressed
in uniform to be presented with my Afghan Service Medal on a
parade. I said no, he got pissed off. 'What is wrong with you? You

will be here and you will be on parade or I will charge you with disobeying a lawful command.' That incident and that MWO just added to my feelings that they did not care about me, it was just the stupid medal which I could care less about, they could mail it to me. But it made me feel like it was a reason to kick me when I was down."

Even by 2012, the Canadian Armed Forces still had not grasped the fact that PTSD is a valid, diagnosable injury resulting from over-seas service, even after hundreds of serving soldiers and veterans had been diagnosed with PTSD related to their service in Bosnia. It was really disheartening that even after being involved for over ten years in Afghanistan, they still had no mandatory training on mental health. The MWO's attitude was a clear example of the lack of education on mental health within the forces, especially within the leadership of the military.

In the end, Jane's doctor intervened and they backed off. Jane left for New Brunswick soon after the head-butt with her bosses. She knew they were glad to see the back of her. They, like so many units in the CAF, had no idea how to support her during her treat-ment and recovery. This was the standard way the CF dealt with problems with personnel who needed support: they just sent the problem away.

"I guess the feeling that many of us felt was that we were now an inconvenience and we took up too much of their time.

"My move east went well and I rented an apartment near the base. I was still fearful and paranoid that my secret would be found out, so I spent 90 percent of my time in my apartment. My link to the outside was through the anonymity of the internet. At some point someone sent me a link to an online military support group called Send Up the Count. Someone must have sensed my fear and thought it was just the stress of being repatriated home from my second tour. I felt that talking on the site might be a way to bleed off some of my stress. So I checked it out, gabbed a bit, and then after a while I felt confident enough to anonymously tell my story.

"Within twenty-four hours of posting that I had been raped over-seas, some I had worked with recognized some of my particulars, especially when I said there was no safe place or anyone I could talk to and I felt suicide was the only way out. I felt that I had taken too big a chance and my fear and paranoia really escalated. I was terri-fied imagining that someone knew what had happened to me. Little did I know that someone had put two and two together and they knew who I was. The person that had recognized me was a former boss of mine that recognized me on the site. She immediately fired off an email to the JPSU at Base Gagetown that I was suicidal.

"I met with the investigators in December 2013, two days after I submitted my complaint. It wasn't easy talking to complete strang-ers about what happened to me. I felt embarrassed and I had a feeling that they thought I was lying or I was embellishing my rape. It was as if I were being raped again. The whole thing was exhausting. It was like scraping a scab off an unhealed wound.

"I felt betrayed. We were always told that they'd take care of you, we've got your back, we're a team, and all the other crap they spill to you especially when you are training to deploy. I believed it and I trusted them that if shit hit the fan, they would be there for me. The opposite occurred. They treated me as if I had done something wrong, yet I was the victim. The way they treated me fuelled my anxiety and shame. I felt useless, used. I had some-thing to be ashamed of. Any progress I felt I had made in dealing with my PTSD disappeared, I spiralled back down into that black hole that my life had fallen into through no fault of my own. I was the one who was being punished.

"So in a matter of months I had lost my career, identity, mar-riage, pride, and my means of income. I couldn't sleep at night because I felt and dreamed that he would come again. I never felt safe and I lived in constant fear. I avoided crowds and my anxiety actually made me physically sick. I avoided going out and I locked myself in my apartment. When I did manage to build the courage to go out, I would get dressed and when I went to open the door, I couldn't. The fear and anxiety would hit me like a hammer. I was so angry that my life had changed so much that I often thought that I'd be better off dead. In the fall and winter 2013/2014 there were a series of suicides by serving soldiers and veterans that made it into the mainstream media. I remember watching the news, listening to the names, and seeing their pictures. I wished I had the courage to kill myself and finally be at peace.

"They told me that they would track the people involved with me before, during, and after I was raped. They said they'd keep me informed of their progress through a victim assistance officer. Within two weeks, they informed me that they had interviewed twelve people and had yet to question the rapist."

So what progress has been made since Jane came forward?

Having served for over thirty years I have had the unfortunate privilege of having to deal with the military police. I can sum up how most soldiers feel about the MP: they are incompetent. The most accurate description I heard someone give of the MPS was, "They are neither military nor are they police."

When Jane and I met in January 2015, she said, "I honestly felt that I would be able to move on and start down the road to recovery and get my life back. The investigation started in December 2013. It is 2015 and the investigators have yet to question my rapist. I was told by my victim assistance officer that he has actually been at Base Gagetown, literally right next to where I live. I could not imagine what I would have done if I had seen him. I'd probably be dead now.

"My weekly email from my victim assistant officer is the same each week. 'The investigation is ongoing.' All that changes is the date. At one point when I questioned why the case was not moving forward, I couldn't believe it when she said they couldn't find him. WHAT? He's still serving and you can't find him? I lost it. I told them I was going to the media, enough was enough. They emailed me and said he was posted to Halifax and was deployed on a ship.

"His life and career were still moving forward and mine was over, no career and no life. In over a year nothing has happened. I feel used, no one cares, and nothing will come of this. He will walk. I know that my rape was not his first and I know that he will rape again. He will go on fucking women's lives up forever. The spectre of suicide is always with me and as this drags on I've actually begun to embrace the thought of ending my life because it actually ended in Afghanistan."

Studies of rape victims consistently report this ratio: for every assault reported and prosecuted there are ten that will never come to light. Soldiers train hard and they deploy on operations as a team, trusting each other with their lives. They also have to trust that the leadership will do everything in their power to protect them from whatever the enemy will throw at them. The last thing that soldiers imagine is that their trauma might come at the hands of a peer or someone in a position of trust.

During my time as a peer support coordinator for the Canadian Armed Forces I met with twelve women who were struggling with an OSI as a direct result of having been sexually assaulted by a peer or superior. Their stories are tragic. I was naive to think that such things never happened. Today I realize that there must have been sexual assaults on my tours. I once assumed that these assaults were dealt with by the chain of command and the perpetrators were severely punished when they were found guilty.

The women I met with looked and sounded empty. There wasn't a spark or even a glimmer of hope in their eyes. When I dealt with women who had been raped I let them decide whether they trusted me enough to hear their story. In some cases it took some time. Regardless, when we did sit and talk, I'd let them control the direction and pace of the conversation. These conversations were like games of chess, back and forth, slowly trying to nail down their source of trauma. Another aspect of a sexual assault OSI, is living in fear as to what might happen if they ever came face to face with the perpetrator. They fear that they may be mentally, physically, or sexually assaulted again even after they return home.

The women I've talked with who have not reported their assault have sometimes ended up working on a day-to-day basis at the same Armed Forces base as their rapist. In some cases they will feign an illness to get away from work and the contact or chance of contact with the person they fear. In many cases, these women have no choice if they feel that they cannot approach their supervisor because of the stigma and fear of reporting their assault. The fear, shame, and anger take over, spiralling down and down until a crisis occurs and they are forced to deal with what has happened to them.

Voluntarily looking for treatment and being diagnosed with an OSI amounts to about 25 percent of your recovery. You have taken a positive step and accepted that something is wrong. Being forced to go see a professional mental health worker when you're not ready can feel like you're being punished, that you have done something wrong, when all you did was serve your country. Therapists have told me that they have attended to women who attempted to blame their OSI on their operational experience such as a close call with an IED or having been shot at and so on, in an effort to disguise the real reason. However, in most cases it doesn't take long for the therapist to realize that the OSI is the result of sexual assault or harassment, and only then will the healing begin.

In 2006, Canada's first female soldier, Captain Nichola Goddard, was killed in combat in Afghanistan. Journalist Valerie Fortney wrote a biography of Goddard entitled *Sunray: The Death and Life of Captain Nichola Goddard* (Key Porter, 2010). In conducting her research, Fortney was given access to private letters that Capt. Goddard had written to her husband that revealed rampant sexual harassment and sexual assault of military women on Canadian bases in Afghanistan. Capt. Goddard wrote, "There were six rapes in the camp last week, so we have to work out an escort at night." The journalist described how

Capt. Goddard tried to "shake off the tension of living in a fortress where men outnumbered women ten to one."

However, from 2004 to 2010, the Canadian military police statistics only list having investigated five reports of sexual harassment or assault in Afghanistan.

There are media reports that a former Canadian military medic has been charged with an additional twenty offences for sexual assault and breach of trust against women at two different bases between 2002 and 2009. In 2011, this medic, Chief Petty Officer James Wilks, was sentenced to only nine months in prison for sexually assaulting three young female recruits. The Department of Defence is now facing a civil suit brought by one of the young women. She claims that the military failed to enforce its policies and monitor its members. It will be legally argued that this protracted failure put her and other women at risk.

The military police have also looked into cases of sexual assault in the youth cadet program (similar to the boy scouts but with a military focus and part of the Forces). The program is open to males and females and it is the young female cadets who are particularly vulnerable under the male chain of command. From 2004 to 2008, there were 219 reported incidents resulting in 156 charges laid for sexual interference, luring a child, sexual assault with a weapon, aggravated sexual assault, invitation to sexual touching, and procuring prostitution. Reported incidents of sexual assault are higher than the adult population of the forces for several reasons, one being the active scrutiny by the cadet leadership and parents for any sign of sexual assault within the program. Even so, officials said the numbers are likely higher because not all cases are reported.

Outside of the military, you could compare this to a teacher or soccer coach sexually assaulting a child in their care. If there were 156 convictions in a similar civilian program, like Scouts Canada, there would be a governmental and RCMP investigation and heads would roll. During my service in the military, both in and out of uniform, I can honestly say that I have never heard even a rumour of such conduct in the cadet program. The system has and still puts a lot of effort into keeping such items out of the media and attempts to deal with it in-house rather than in the criminal courts, under public scrutiny.

In 2009, the Canadian Military Police Criminal Intelligence Program noted a dramatic increase in domestic violence—100 incidents reported each year in 2007 and 2008—that coincided with military personnel returning from Afghanistan. The military police recommended that the Department of National Defence conduct a review. In January 2011, the Canadian Forces Provost Marshal (head cop for the CF) released an internal report on criminal charges filed against soldiers and civilians associated with the military that revealed a high rate of sexual assaults against children, and child pornography.

However, according to a spokesperson for the Canadian Forces Provost Marshal and the Canadian Forces National Investigation Service (NIS), in the years since 2004, the Canadian military admits to having investigated only five reports of sexual assault in Afghanistan. Only one investigation led to a guilty verdict. The Canadian Forces Provost Marshal then goes on to state that there were 170 sexual assaults in the military in 2008, a drop from the 176 reported in 2007 and 201 in 2006. But the statistics are not broken down into sexual assaults on operations and those committed in Canada. The military police get as many as 200 complaints of sexual assault each year, with many more cases going unreported because the victims fear the consequences within the military hierarchy of coming forward. It is obvious that information on the prevalence of sexual assault on Canada's military deployments and on its bases is not as accurate as it is made out to be.

When a person joins the Forces, the job comes with many hidden tolls and sacrifices. Freedom of speech, safety, long periods of time away, family disruption, and so on. However, sexual assault continues to be the most difficult to deal with at all levels of the military. And even after all of the internal reports from the judge advocate, the military police, and military and civilian ombudsmen, the Department of National Defence still claims that incidents of sexual harassment and assault are minimal.

Though the DND does have directives against sexual misconduct and harassment, and has training and awareness programs, the problems persist. Its mandatory "programs" are one-shot deals. An example of one of these was the implementation of a harassment policy, for which I received a single briefing. The main excuse for not carrying out any annual training was there was no time available for such touchy-feely programs. Once the mandatory training on subjects like harassment, mental health, and violence against women are completed, any follow-up training is at the discretion of commanding officers. And there is no accountability or consequences for the chain of command if such training is not carried out within their units.

At some point in the 1980s, the military enacted a policy that any claims of sexual assault were to be dealt with through the chain of command. During my thirty-two years of service, I never knew that such a policy existed. I always assumed that sexual assault was a federal offence, reported to the civilian authorities, and dealt with by the court. Not so—in most cases it is dealt with internally. A fair comparison that has come to light in recent years is the way the church has dealt with pedophile priests. Rather than reported, they were dealt with internally and the perpetrator simply moved somewhere else. As with the church, the military has a history of protecting its leadership at all costs.

In 2012, *The Invisible War*, a very poignant documentary about sexual assault in the American military, was released and has had a direct impact on US military policy. The film was viewed by US Secretary of Defence Leon Panetta who immediately threw out the policy of allowing the chain of command to deal with sexual assault within its ranks.

Here at home, the Canadian military will do what it does amazingly well: they will look into it, study it, asses it, form a committee to come to grips with it. Then, to add credibility to their looking in to it, they will hire an independent civilian consulting firm that will confirm the obvious: that there is a systemic problem with sexual assault in the Forces. Once the obvious is confirmed, they will proceed as they have with OSIs and the mental health of their soldiers. There will be no decisive decision or an executive order from on high to deal with the problem. Don't get me wrong, the leadership will posture, pose, be alarmed, and promise that sexual assault will be dealt with, that it will not tolerated, and that those found guilty will be prosecuted. In reality, they will ignore it, knowing "it" will eventually lose traction with the media and quietly go away.

There is no doubt an invisible war is raging in the Canadian military. It is comprised of sexual harassment, sexual assault, domestic violence, child abuse, and child pornography. The military's patriarchy and hierarchy make it an institution that is susceptible to violence against women, which creates an environment which is not safe for women. Research shows that sexual violence is the primary factor for PTSD among female soldiers. For their male counterparts, the strongest PTSD predictor is combat experience. Think about that. The women on these operational tours are more afraid of their peers than they are of the Taliban.

You would be wrong to think that a sexual assault would come at the hands of one of the combat soldiers returning from being outside the wire, in the shit. No, the combat soldiers were more concerned about eating, sleeping, and washing their bodies and clothes. For them, it was about staying alive and getting home in one piece. No, the majority of sexual assaults happened in the static units where everyone was living comfortably and never left the safety of the large bases.

In cases where the assault was reported, the Canadian military refused to take action, silencing the survivors of sexual assault and sweeping accusations under the rug. The last thorough airing of sexual assault in a military context in Canada was more than a decade ago, in 1998. Recently, however, the country's top military commander has been called to a parliamentary committee to answer questions about reports of sexual violence in the military.

The media reported that General Tom Lawson, Chief of Defence Staff, was grilled by the Standing Committee on Defence & Veterans Affairs about recent media reports claiming that sexual assaults within the ranks are at an epidemic level. Lawson testified that an internal review carried out since the claims were first reported has identified "some barriers" that prevent alleged victims from coming forward. Military officials who testified alongside Lawson pointed out that there have been instances when the accused and their alleged victims have been moved around after a complaint has been filed. In some rare circumstances, when the accused is a commanding officer, the individual has been relieved of duty. Out of twelve recent assault cases tried by the military justice system, there has been only one conviction.

In 2009 the Federal Office of the Ombudsman for Victims of Crime determined that it had sufficient evidence to include a section on Sexual Violence & Harassment in the ranks of Canada's armed forces. In his report, the Ombudsman recommended to the Minister of National Defence that the total level of sexual violence in the military be more accurately determined for both reported and unreported cases, and that there be a thorough review of existing educational programs on what constitutes sexual assault and what supports are available for victims. This is more evidence that there is a problem in the military, but the recommendation itself can, and in all likelihood will, be ignored. The leadership of the forces see this recommendation as meddling into the treatment of members of the military who have experienced sexual assault during their service and the leadership chooses to ignore the facts.

The women I spoke to said that even if I changed their names in the book, they would still be afraid of being identified. Some are just beginning to have their complaint dealt with by the military police, while others who have not registered a complaint have said that they just want it all to go away. I tell them that it won't, that it will haunt them for the rest of their lives and in coming forward, they will change the way they live their lives.

I cannot bring myself to use words like disturbed, upset, dismayed, concerned, when I talk about sexual assault in the military, because these are words used by the shit-deflectors to sugar-coat and minimize the problem when addressing the media. No, my words are from a soldier's and a veteran's view of these crimes against the women in the military: I am fucking angry that these crimes occur and are half-heartedly dealt with because we are all painted with the same brush and in the court of public opinion we are all rapists.

The real perpetrators are the military leadership who have chosen to ignore the problem and allow the rapists to go unpunished rather than provide a safe environment for its members, especially for women. The Canadian Armed Forces is marred by a sexualized culture that disproportionately affects lower-ranking female members, most of whom do not report the wrongdoings, as a sweeping report has found.

Still, Canada's top military officer refused to promise to enact the main recommendation in the hard-hitting report, namely the creation of a fully independent agency to receive complaints of inappropriate sexual conduct and offer support to victims of assault and harassment.

In June 2015 Chief of the Defence Staff General Tom Lawson said in a CBC interview that sexual harassment is still an issue in the Canadian Forces because people are "biologically wired in a certain way." It would be a trite answer, but it's because we're biologically wired in a certain way and there will be those who believe it is a reasonable thing to press themselves and their desires on others.

Lawson quickly backpedalled and apologized for what he called an "awkward characterization." He went on to say the "terrible issue" of military sexual harassment "disturbs the great majority of everyone in uniform and yet, we're still dealing with it. Much as we would very much like to be absolutely professional in everything we do, and I think by and large we are, there will be situations and have been situations where, largely, men will see themselves as able to press themselves onto our women members."

These are the comments of the leader of the Canadian Armed Forces. I felt sorry for the victims of sexual assault when I heard his words translated into soldier speak: ignore it and it will go away. There is no support or safety net for the victims of sexual assault in the Canadian Armed Forces, and it looks like it will not be forthcoming.

The CAF, for some reason, always seems to be slow to get off the mark when problems such as sexual assault come to the surface. The United States, Australia, and European countries such as France have already created organizations that are outside of the chain of command to counteract the reluctance of victims to come forward with complaints to their superiors. My question is why the Canadian military is so resistant to sorting out why sexual assault is not taken seriously? I guess the leadership mantra "Know your troops and promote their welfare" is, in the end, just empty words.

CHAPTER 17
SUICIDE

S ince the end of the combat operations in Afghanistan in 2011 and the complete withdrawal of the Canadian contingent in 2014, there has been an alarming rise in suicides among serving soldiers, reservists, and veterans. The rise in suicides points to a system that is failing in its duty to take care of its people.

Over a three-month period, from November 2013 to January 2014, there were ten suicides of serving soldiers and veterans. When reporting the suicide rate in the armed forces, attempted suicides are not factored into the equation. In my opinion, including them would offer a clearer picture.

Veterans Affairs does not keep statistics on the rate of attempted suicides and suicides in veterans' communities. The leadership in the armed forces and the government also claims that the reasons for suicides are difficult to relate to someone's service especially on operations, which casts doubt on the overall suicide rate in the Forces. On July 5, 2014, the forces released a report to the media stating that, of the ten suicides over a four-month period in late 2013 and early 2014, only three of the victims had been diagnosed with PTSD. So the system can breathe a sigh of relief because the statistics back them up. Regardless of their individual reasons, ten members of the forces ended up in a state where the only answer to their problems was to end their life. If this were the RCMP, the Canadian Coast Guard, or prison guards, if any organization lost ten of their employees in a four-month period it would definitely be a very big cause for concern. Instead, the Forces' concern was establishing that the reasons for these deaths was not military service. It boils down to covering their asses and protecting the system instead of taking care of troops.

Many veterans also feel that the government is playing with the statistics and in doing so, have created an environment of distrust amongst those ill and injured from operations in Afghanistan, Bosnia, Rwanda, and so on. A recent multimillion-dollar ad campaign, with full-page ads in national newspapers and prime time spots during the Stanley Cup playoffs is a ridiculous waste of money, especially when VAC is closing offices in a ham-handed attempt to make veterans look like a bunch of whiners. The young veterans of today are made to look like all they are focused on is getting as much money as they can out of Veterans Affairs. The talking points that have been written for the politicians highlight all of the programs and financial support available for severely injured veterans. For those veterans who fall below this poorly defined "severely injured" line, it is extremely difficult to navigate through the paperwork and crap that is the norm for Veterans Affairs and most government departments.

We will probably never know how many suicides and attempted suicides were a result of getting jerked around by the system. I have talked with employees in Veterans Affairs who have said, "Why do we make it so difficult for veterans to access entitlements?" Veterans feel that it is a "we-versus-them" environment and an adversarial way of doing business. Over the past few years many veterans have come to feel that they have done something wrong and are being punished—we're just not sure what for. As one veteran told me, "If they're going to make me feel that I've done something wrong, you'd think they'd at least have the decency to tell me what I've done."

Suicide in the military has always been a dark aspect of serving your country. The military has chosen to keep the incidents of suicide off the radar screen especially when it comes to the media.

A recent study on the causes of death for former members of the CF provides initial estimates to indicate the extent of the problem. The following data is for those who enrolled in the Regular Force after 1972, and were released prior to December 31, 2007:

- Men (total of 96,786): 2,620 had died, 696 (26.6 percent) by suicide.
- Women (total of 15,439): 204 had died, 29 (14 percent) by suicide.

During my thirty-two years of service, there were several suicides I can't forget. The first was very early in my career as a soldier. He was a corporal in the rifle company I served with in the early '70s. I had about two years in the army at that time. One Monday when we were formed up for roll call, once the heads were counted, our company commander dismissed us and said to gather around him. We hushed up, he cleared his throat, and said that Corporal Marks had committed suicide over the weekend.

"What?" Then disbelief: "Is he really dead?" He was. He had left behind a wife and three children. I had no idea of what to say or how to react. I looked at the guys around me but most looked like me. They were shocked.

As the shock wore off, I realized that I and another fellow were probably the last guys to have seen him before he killed himself. It was on Friday evening, and we met him in the canteen as he was coming down the stairs and he was very drunk. That Friday was the first day he had been allowed back into the canteen after having been barred for four months for fighting. He was staggering drunk and as he weaved his way down the stairs we laughed and asked him, "Where you going?"

"I'm going home to kill myself. I've had enough of this crap."

We laughed as he turned and stumbled down the last few stairs. In hindsight, feeling guilty, I asked myself why those words had sounded like a joke. But he was a real joker, always funny and quick with a witty answer to any question. Back then, suicide was a taboo subject. There was no suicide intervention training, and even if there were, there would have been little interest in it, the attitude towards suicide being that it was just part of the job.

Later in the day we heard some of the details. After meeting us on the steps, Mark had left the canteen, caught a taxi, and gone home. He went inside and found his .30-30 hunting rifle, loaded it, then went and sat on the sofa in the tiny living room of his military family accommodation. He slid off of the sofa and ended up sitting on the floor leaning against the sofa. This commotion woke his family. His wife knew he would be drunk so she cautiously made her way down the stairs. She knew what he was up to but the other times he had threatened to blow his head off had ended up with him sobbing on her shoulder as she led him upstairs and put him to bed. This time it was different. His voice was clear and cold. She sensed that he was serious and she was scared. She pleaded with him, tried to reason with him, but to no avail. By then, unknown to her, the kids had made their way to the stairs and were peering over the railing taking in what was going on in the living room. It was all very quick. He placed to barrel of the rifle under his chin and pulled the trigger. He blew the top and most of the back of his skull off. He had made his choice.

On that Monday we all struggled to find a reason as to why he had killed himself. Was it the booze? Was it his family life? Or was he sick? We needed an answer.

Later in the day after we were dismissed, I made my way back to the barracks with the question rolling around in my head. What had taken over by then was the guilt. Why had I not noticed? The intervention scenarios came rolling out and the what-ifs. If I had done this or that maybe he'd be still alive.

The next day as we gathered for the ritual roll call, the death of Marks was the only thing that we talked about. I listened and eventually recounted my meeting him at the canteen and what he'd said. I should have intervened, I said, and an older soldier replied, "Yeah, if your auntie had a dick she'd be your uncle."

We buried him a few days later with full military honours because in the book on how to conduct a funeral, there is no scenario for burying someone who has taken their own life. The service was held at a small church where his wife was from, just outside of Fredericton. The church was one of those small, white, lonely, out of the way churches you see on the back roads of any province. The day was cold, rainy, and very sombre. It was as if someone had written a script for this funeral service. The whole company was there, along with the various higher ranks. The family filled the first rows of pews and the hundred plus of us sat if we could or stood in the back against the wall, crammed in like sardines.

The service began with the various incantations and readings by the padre. "There by the grace of God." The words sounded hollow, with a taste of disgust, because they were being said for someone who had sinned by killing himself. Over the years, I would come to realize that the words of the service never changed, and that that line always seemed to contain the disgust and bitterness I heard at that first funeral.

When it came time for the padre to say a few words about Marks I was shocked when he immediately lashed out at the family, blaming them for Marks's death: "If you would have been more attentive, understanding, and forgiving, he would be with us still." The family, already shattered by the suicide, began to cry and moan. But the dipshit padre kept piling it on. I was not the only one who was thinking, Who the fuck is this guy? Shut the fuck up and finish this ritual so I can get outside, so I can breathe, and we can put him into the ground.

Eventually the padre finished his tirade and finished off with some loving and caring words. We burst out of the church and sorted ourselves into the carrying party (pall bearers), firing party, escorts (I was one), and then the family. The cemetery was right next to the church, perched on a little hillock, and the rain had turned the uphill entrance into a slippery slope. The carrying party was slipping and sliding and at one point they came close to dropping the casket. The pallbearers dug in and finally managed to get to the grave, which was half full of water. What now, I thought? The army being the epitome of flexibility carried on with the casket resting on the lowering straps. The Company Sergeant Major said that the casket would remain in the vault and Marks would be interred at a later date. The firing party fired the salute, the sound of the rifle fire bouncing off the low clouds and the surrounding valley, triggering the rain, and it poured. The rain put an end to the proceedings and everyone beat a hasty retreat to their cars and us to our buses. It was quiet in the bus, all the smokers lit up. We drove away and left the family to grieve and wonder why.

Looking out of the window as we drove through the rain-soaked countryside, I went over what I had just witnessed. It was a sad, angry, and in my view, confusing ceremony that left me wondering if we had really, as they say today, "celebrated the life" of Corporal Marks. This would not be my last brush with suicide. There would be many more to come.

There was the military police sergeant who came to work one day, went into his office, and blew his brains out with his service pistol.

The young soldier going through his training to become a tank driver. He did not like the army life, and sitting alone in the phone booth he told his girlfriend, "I just want to go home." In his lonely, confused state he felt that the only way to get out of the army was to kill himself. He said goodbye to his girlfriend, said he loved her, and hung up. She knew that he was serious and tried to contact someone at the base. She eventually did, and the duty officer and the military police raced to the barracks, but they were too late. They found him slumped over dead in the phone booth in the foyer of the barracks.

A combat engineer in Oromocto, NB (where Base Gagetown is), was talking with his wife who was visiting her parents in Quebec City. He was caught up in his nightmare of being diagnosed with PTSD and was rarely calm when he spoke with his wife. But what really caused concern for her was when he said, "Tell the kids I love them" just before he hung up. Without hesitating, she called the RCMP. The police station was right across the street from their house. When the police kicked down the door they found him at death's door but alive. He was rushed to the hospital and they managed to pump his stomach out and stop the cocktail of prescription drugs from killing him. A close call. One of the ones the Forces does not publish in their annual report on suicides.

When I served with the 3rd Battalion of the RCR, stationed in Winnipeg at the time, there were several attempts and a few successful suicides. One soldier who should never have been in the army, let alone in the infantry, went to the middle of one of the bridges over the Red River. When he jumped, the river was low and he ended up crashing into the riverbank. His injuries were significant and he saved his own life by crawling up the bank into an apartment parking lot where he was found covered in mud and about to lose consciousness due to hypothermia. You would have thought that his close brush with death would have motivated him to get help. He was sent to the National Defence Medical Centre in Ottawa for treatment. It did not matter; he wanted to die. He managed to get out of the secure ward, and was found dead not far from the hospital.

Another soldier in Winnipeg failed to report for duty one Monday morning, which was not uncommon, there were always a few that slept in after a weekend of partying. There were those who had hooked up with one of the so-called "whiskey dollies" that hung out at the bars frequented by soldiers and bikers. However, by early afternoon, his platoon warrant officer sent a couple of fellows to the absent soldier's apartment. Arriving there, they knew that something was wrong because of the smell at the door. They called the police, and when they entered they found him dead from a shotgun blast to the head. They said he probably killed himself on Friday and had already started to decompose. Later in the week the coroner confirmed it had been suicide. The unit picked up the body and had it shipped to his family for burial. When I look back, I realize why the unit did not even hold a memorial service or mark the death of this soldier: he had taken the "easy way" out.

After I was released from the Forces, I was hired by National Defence and Veterans Affairs as a peer support coordinator to work with soldiers and veterans who were suffering with PTSD. I met one of my first peers after seeing the front-page photo in the Fredericton *Daily Gleaner*. There he was in the almost ice-covered St. John River, being rescued by the fire department. When I met him in the psych ward a few days later he still wished he'd died and ended the psychological torment he was in.

Rank did not make a soldier immune to suicide. You would think that with more years of service and experience, a higher ranking soldier would be better armed against the path to suicide.

A chief warrant officer (CWO) is the highest rank you can achieve outside of being an officer. In an infantry battalion of several hundred soldiers, there is only one CWO. So when an up-and-coming young CWO that we all knew was missing we were surprised and shocked to hear who it was. He was about forty, fit, motivated, a skilled athlete, intelligent, and a poster boy for young soldiers to emulate.

He did not show up for work on a Monday morning, which did not cause any concern because at his rank level no one kept tabs on his coming and goings. However, by Tuesday when he was not at his accommodation and there was no response on his cell phone, the search was on. At the time of his disappearance he was posted to Base Kingston, Ontario, and his family was still back in Base Gagetown. They contacted his wife and he was not at home. The military police and the RCMP began the search and through his credit card transactions they tracked him to a hotel in Ireland.

When the local police found him in the hotel he had hanged himself in the closet. Why kill himself in Ireland? He was third-generation Irish and, we found out later, he had always wanted to visit the old country.

There were many more, some I knew, others on the base I was serving at. Many were kept under wraps. You would see the flag at half-mast at the main gate and wonder who had died. It would be years before the attitude "they took the easy way out" would change. I eventually changed my view on suicide. Now I felt guilty because it meant we had not noticed the signs and if we did we had failed to intervene.

In the Forces, suicide still elicits a feeling that the soldier was weak and succumbed: it is not the system's fault. This attitude was apparent when I attended the funeral of a warrant officer from my former regiment who committed suicide. I knew him by name but never met him. Regardless, he was a soldier who ended up in a suicidal state and no one recognized his pleas for help. I was told that the signs were there, yet no one acted on them. I expected the funeral would be well attended but I was shocked when I saw the base chapel half empty. There were a few of the soldiers who worked with him and the required brass were there because they had to be.

The standard words were said, the family cried and mourned their loss. It seemed to last just a few moments. I stood at the back of the chapel as the family and the military filed out and what I saw on their faces was "get me the hell out of here." The service was the minimum that was required by the military and those who attended were only those required to. This was a dishonourable death if there is such a thing. I felt sad and angry. I thought the Forces had turned the page on suicide and that they saw it as a tragic, preventable kind of death, but no, it was still seen as a sign of weakness to "take the easy way out."

One of the statistics noted by the CF is that the percentage of deaths attributable to suicide is at least 50 percent lower among those who remained with the CF. The CF conveniently rolls out and stands by a percentage that they say is comparable to the suicide rate in the civilian population. The percentages cannot be argued; they are correct. However, they only count those who committed suicide while serving. No one is tracking the attempted suicides, nor do they track suicides of soldiers who were released from the CF. Veterans Affairs Canada does not track suicides in the veteran population! In short, the number of suicides related to service in the CF can be massaged to suit the system.

The deaths will continue. The stigma related to suicide has not lessened, and soldiers and veterans are still reluctant to seek help. In their minds there is no other way out of the situation and in a strange way they see suicide as the honourable exit. It is impossible to know how many are just a trigger pull away from ending their lives. How many were pulled away from the edge by a phone call or a child's words unknowingly breaking the trance.

The numbers are still being manipulated by the bean-counters in the system and they continue to blow smoke up the public's ass and deflect the fact that there is a big problem with suicide in the forces.

Recently, there was a small item in the obituaries of our local paper that marked the first anniversary of the death of a peer I had worked with through OSISS.

Ray contacted me from the transition facility for men who are released from prison and are awaiting parole. He had just finished a two-year sentence for the robbery of a Subway restaurant. At the time, he had been on a drug and booze binge for several days and he needed money to feed his addictions. We met several times and he attended our support group for soldiers and veterans, but I knew there was something that just wasn't right.

It came to light when he disappeared for several months and I received no word. When we did make contact, he said he had been staying with relatives in a small town nearby. I immediately knew that he was stoned and he was stoned every time I met with him. What really messed with me were the lies and bullshit he spewed whenever we talked. I know it was the drugs talking. Regardless I kept repeating the mantra I used with fellows who had addictions: "Get off the booze/drugs, get into therapy, and take your medications." I realize that it is not that easy. In fact, it is far from easy to get the demons off your back, but there was nothing else I could say. The ball is always in their court.

Recently, national news outlets (NPR [January 14, 2013], BBC [July 14, 2013], *Edmonton Sun* [September 16, 2014], *The Star* [September 16, 2014]) have stated that since 2002 there have been more suicides on year-by-year basis in the CAF than there were soldiers killed during operations in Afghanistan. Between 2002 to 2012 deaths due to operations in Afghanistan: 158. Suicides during the same period: 178. The United States is also losing veterans at an alarming rate due to suicide. The same is going on in the United Kingdom, where suicide deaths in the military and among veterans has surpassed the number killed in Iraq and Afghanistan.

Whenever the rate of suicide is questioned, the CAF has always said the rate is equivalent to the rate in the general public. These figures are not accurate because suicides by women in the CAF and in the reserves are not factored in. It is sad that the CAF and the government go out of their way to manipulate and minimize the facts—and to suit what?

SUICIDES IN THE CANADIAN ARMED FORCES, 2004 TO MARCH 31, 2014
Source: Department of National Defence

2014 (up to March 31)
Male, regular forces: 5
Female, regular forces: 0
Male and female reserves: 3
Total: 8

2013
Male, regular forces: 9
Female, regular forces: 1
Male and female reserves: 3
Total: 13

2012
Male, regular forces: 10
Female, regular forces: 3
Male and female reserves: 4
Total: 17

2011
Male, regular forces: 21
Female, regular forces: 1
Male and female reserves: 3
Total: 25

2010
Male, regular forces: 12
Female, regular forces: 0
Male and female reserves: 1
Total: 13

2009
Male, regular forces: 12
Female, regular forces: 2
Male and female reserves: 8
Total: 22

2008
Male, regular forces: 13
Female, regular forces: 1
Male and female reserves: 1
Total: 15

2007
Male, regular forces: 9
Female, regular forces: 1
Male and female reserves: 2
Total: 12

2006
Male, regular forces: 7
Female, regular forces: 1
Male and female reserves: 3
Total: 11

2005
Male, regular forces: 10
Female, regular forces: 0
Male and female reserves: 1
Total: 11

2004
Male, regular forces: 10
Female, regular forces: 0
Male and female reserves: 3
Total: 13

EPILOGUE

In 2000 I was diagnosed with severe chronic PTSD. I've been on medication since then and I see a therapist every two weeks. It has been a long and extremely challenging road to finding peace. However, perseverance has paid off and I feel like I've got my life back. Overcoming my denial that I had PTSD was really difficult to admit, as was my guilt about surviving Bosnia, which still rears its head from time to time.

Today when the guilt comes, it is in the form of not having been able to serve in Afghanistan. I wanted to do my part and be there with the troops. As the casualties grew so did my guilt, especially when friends like Chief Warrant Officer Bobby Girouard and Sergeant Robert Short were killed. I fell into a pit depression and I just wanted stay there. Most of the dead were so young with so much to live for. My guilt has, in a perverse way, caused me to think that I would have changed places with anyone of them. I've had a good life so why shouldn't they?

I have attended several memorial services for the fallen and it rips the guts out of me every time. It's like I am punishing myself. It is so difficult to keep my emotions in check especially when I see the families wrapped in a quilt of grief. At these services I am able hold it together and be the tough soldier, knowing my tears will come later when I'm alone.

The work I've done as a peer support coordinator with the OSISS program has brought me face to face with soldiers and veterans who have served in Afghanistan. After almost ten years with the program, I began to feel that I had nothing in common with their service in Afghanistan. My experience and injury from Bosnia and my story felt very dated. I could no longer say, "I understand," because I didn't. Their experiences were so different from mine and the closest thing I could say was, "I can only imagine." Many of the veterans that I have dealt with have not served in Afghanistan and they have said the same thing, that they "feel guilty every time they hear of the death of a soldier in Afghanistan. We're safe at home. Yet we feel we still had something to give.

Personally, I feel embarrassed whenever I talk with someone who has served in Afghanistan. This guilt really strikes close to home. My son, Ben, has been to Afghanistan five times and I find it extremely difficult to talk to him about his experiences. Regardless of my guilt, I can honestly say that OSISS and my part in it has saved lives. The greatest reward I have ever received is hearing, "Fred, if it weren't for you I'd be dead now."

Even with my misplaced (as my psychologist calls it) guilt, my life is filled with more satisfaction and happiness than I could have ever imagined, and after forty-two years of service with the Canadian Armed Forces, I only have three regrets:

1. I should have put more effort into joining the French Foreign Legion in 1969.
2. I should have kicked the shit out of a certain R22R warrant officer at the Airborne Centre for being an asshole.
3. I should have kicked the shit out of a certain master corporal who, on New Year's Eve 1972, sent the military police to my place with an order for me to be at the Officers' Mess New Year's Party. So instead of Janice and I spending our

first New Year's together as a married couple, I took a taxi to the Officers' Mess, and opened car doors for the gentlemen and their wives. When they had all arrived, I went to work inside bussing tables. I spent New Year's 1973 as part of the UN mission in Cyprus. It wasn't until 1974 that we rang in the New Year together.

Not bad for four decades of service. My PTSD has made me realize that holding a grudge and fuelling anger requires a lot of energy which, in the end, is wasted. I now know that life is too short to waste your time on crap like anger. Life is not a reusable resource. You only get one kick at it, so make the best of it.

Pro Patria.

ACKNOWLEDGEMENTS

First are the veterans and soldiers who have allowed me to write and tell their stories. Thank you.

I wish to thank my family, who have been outstanding over the past fifteen years—thank you for being there for me. Janice, who has poked me in the ribs to "get to work on the book" and who now keeps asking me, "When are you going to be finished with the book?" You are a great friend and partner. You have such a kind heart and really care for the ones you love.

Ben, Terri, and Erin, who understand what soldiering is all about. And my little free-range, all-natural anti-depressants, the grandbrats: Ethan, Amos, and Logan. I can never be down when you guys are around. I love you.

I wish to thank my peers at OSISS Team Atlantic who I consider friends more than just colleagues: the "ladies" who work tirelessly with the families of the injured—Nadine de Blois, Wanda Lewis, Jenny Fairbank, Danielle Boudreau, and Amanda Carlisle—you are all priceless. My fellow PSCS: Steve Hurley, Dave McArdle (Happy 100th), Jerry Deveau, Tim Elliot—take care of yourselves. Owen Parkhouse, who has moved on to (hopefully) instill some "common good" at the Veterans Review & Appeal Board.

Jerry Deveau, a friend and colleague who was a joy to work with even though he's a combat engineer. Fellow Royal Glenn Park, who effectively filled the void when I moved on. Fred Leblanc and Ian Cable for being true good friends and all of my fellow veterans in the Blue Helmets. Also to all of the peers who have attended the support group over the years, I hope it helped.

Shawn Hearn for his loyalty to the program and his peers in the Atlantic Region, take care of yourself.

Kathy Darte for all of her work on the VAC side of the program, you are missed.

Lisa Murphy for her sense of humour, solid work, support of the program, and for giving the men in OSISS the great image of going "commando"! It made the boring parts of our conferences tolerable.

Juan Cargnello for being a really nice guy and refereeing our self-care sessions and for the great work he has done with the training of volunteers. Juan, do you still comb your hair with a hand grenade?

Lieutenant Colonel Stephan Grenier for having the vision and the tenacity to make the program work. We veterans and soldiers thank you.

Michelle Jubinville and Lise Bourque, the two VAC "Angels" employed at Base Gagetown, you may never know how caring and important your work has been for me. Your understanding, kindness, and concern has proven to be an invaluable resource to veterans and soldiers. I thank you.

Robin Geneau and Joyce Belliveau, therapists who went to bat for soldiers who were not receiving the therapy they were entitled to. Your efforts were not in vain—things have changed. Also, to all of the therapists who, through their guidance and support, have given so many soldiers, veterans, and their families their lives back.

Last but not least Patrick Murphy and the staff at Nimbus, I thank you for allowing me to tell these stories.